Chessercizes

BRUCE PANDOLFINI

A FIRESIDE BOOK
Published by Simon & Schuster Inc.

NEW YORK   LONDON   TORONTO   SYDNEY   TOKYO   SINGAPORE

Fireside

Simon & Schuster Building
Rockefeller Center
1230 Avenue of the Americas
New York, New York 10020

Copyright © 1991 by Bruce Pandolfini

FIRESIDE and colophon are registered trademarks
of Simon & Schuster Inc.

Designed by Stanley S. Drate/Folio Graphics Co. Inc.

Manufactured in the United States of America

10   9   8   7   6   5   4   3   2   1   Pbk.

Library of Congress Cataloging in Publication Data

Pandolfini, Bruce.
    Chessercizes / Bruce Pandolfini.
        p.   cm.
    "A Fireside book."
    Includes index.
    1. Chess—Collections of games.   2. Chess—Study and teaching.
    I. Title.
    GV1452.P33   1991   90-13827
    794.1'6—dc20   CIP
    ISBN 0-671-70184-3 Pbk.

For Idelle

Acknowledgments

I would like to thank Bruce Alberston, Idelle Pandolfini, Carol Ann Caronia, Larry Tamarkin, Burt Hochberg, Renée Rabb, Sean Devlin, Christopher Shea, Bonni Leon, Laura Yorke, André Bernard, and my editor Kara Leverte.

My appreciation must also go to Lisa Adler, Bret Agins, Matt Bacal, Alec Diacou, Wills Hapworth, Jason and Philip Kalisman, David and Deborah Newman, Morgan Pehme, Nathania and Jacob Rubin, Tony Rykowski, Robert Sinn, David Slifka, Josh Waitzkin, Pam Wasserstein, David Yourdon, and David Zindel for their analysis.

Contents

Introduction

Chessercizes is a book of one hundred instructive contemporary tactics, all selected from outstanding tournament and match games played in 1989 by masters and grandmasters. You'll find examples by World Champion Garry Kasparov and former champ Anatoly Karpov, along with combinations by today's prominent challengers for the top spot. Many of the tactics were played in such major tournaments as national championships and world cup events, and reflect the highest competitive standards. You'll also find combinations by tomorrow's stars, including Hungary's Polgar sisters, Russia's Vassily Ivanchuk, and America's brilliant young prodigy Gata Kamsky. All may someday vie for the world championship.

The examples represent the full richness of the modern combination, many of them offering several different themes woven into tactical complexities. *Chessercizes* first arranges these themes into separate chapters and then points out in each example where a specific tactic occurs.

Chessercizes is really two books in one. Part One is a collection of one hundred carefully chosen examples, arranged in order of difficulty. This section is aimed at the average player. If positions prove a little too tough for newcomers, Part Two, including "Little Chessercizes," distills the essence of the examples in

Part One into simpler patterns, using only the key pieces and pawns. To let you practice setting up diagrams by following algebraic notation, the examples in Part Two are given in notation only instead of being pictured in diagrams.

Suppose you have difficulty solving Part One's Chessercize number 4, for instance. Simply turn to Part Two, "Little Chessercizes," beginning on page 187. There, under the corresponding number 4, you'll find its basic patterns (in this case two of them, 4a and 4b). These examples relate directly to problem 4 in Part One. To help you focus on the truly relevant aspects of the problem, each "Little Chessercize" shows only its key themes, with just the necessary pieces on the board. Moreover, each "little" problem can be solved in one move.

After solving these simplified versions and checking the answers in the accompanying answer section of Part Two, you can turn back to Part One knowing what to look for and be prepared to understand the more complex forms of the same themes.

The "Little Chessercizes" should be helpful not only to beginners but also to parents and teachers— even to strong players. Many of the game's leading grandmasters, such as former world champion Mikhail Tal, have been known to study beginners' lessons, perhaps to strengthen fundamental concepts, or for the benefit of their students, or just to get another perspective on things too easily taken for granted.

Chessercizes has eight main chapters. Because checkmate is the chief goal of a chess game, mating nets are presented as the book's first theme. Checkmate is also the easiest tactic to comprehend.

A mating net, or pattern, is a forced mate, which means there is no way for the defender to avoid quick checkmate against correct play. Chapter One offers fourteen mating nets, arranged in a graduated sequence from simple to more complex. Thus, number 5 should be harder to solve than number 1.

Chapters Two and Three deal with mating attacks. A mating attack differs from a mating net in that mate can be averted, though often only by sacrificing material. A mating attack is a general assault against the king, usually involving several cooperating units and resulting in mate or significant gain of material. Chapter Two (examples 15–30) offers mating attacks against the uncastled king. The defending king in these situations is stuck in the center or has been lured out of hiding. Chapter Three (examples 31–47) presents mating attacks against castled king fortresses, where the defender has already sought safety for his king.

Chapter Four (examples 48–59) introduces the first of the nonmating tactics: forks and double attacks. A fork is a threat by one unit against two or more enemy units simultaneously.

Chapter Five offers nine pinning combinations (examples 60–68). A pin is an attack on a piece that shields a more valuable piece. Since the pinned piece can't or shouldn't move, it tends to be vulnerable to additional attacks.

Chapter Six offers six problems (examples 69–74) on skewers and discoveries. A skewer is similar to a pin in that it is directed against two enemy pieces on the same line. But unlike a pin, now the more valuable piece is first in the line of attack and must move away, exposing the piece behind it to capture. A discovery is an attack by a stationary piece "discovered" when another piece of the same color moves out of its way, off the line of attack.

Chapter Seven (examples 75–88) presents three separate tactical concepts: overloads, removing the guard, and deflections. A piece is overloaded when it unsuccessfully attempts to defend two or more points at the same time. A guard for a piece can be removed by capturing it or driving it away. A deflection occurs when a protecting piece is forced out of position so that it no longer provides defense.

Chapter Eight (examples 89–100) offers a melange

of tactics in the endgame, the final phase. Here, the key theme is usually the promotion of a pawn into a queen. Once you obtain an extra queen, mate cannot be far away.

Chessercizes can be read from the start, or, especially if you want to concentrate on specific tactics, in sections. Each problem follows the same format: identification of the players, etc.; a problem diagram; and an explanation. You might want to keep a tally of your correct answers and compare yourself to other levels of rated chessplayers, as given here:

A USCF (United States Chess Federation) 2400 player (a strong master) might get all 100 correct.
A master player rated 2200 might get 90 right.
An expert rated 2100 might get 80 right.
A 2000 player might get 70 right.
And so on down the line.

A rated 1400 player should get at least 10 problems right. You be the judge on partial solutions. I suggest giving half a point for each almost correct answer.

The tactics presented in Chessercizes can be employed on many levels. After all, the book was inspired by the game's foremost exponents as they engaged in important tournaments and matches worldwide.

The next move is yours.

Algebraic Notation

To read Chessercizes you will need a knowledge of algebraic notation.

The board is an eight-by-eight grid of sixty-four squares arranged in ranks and files. Ranks are horizontal rows of squares, numbered 1 through 8, beginning from White's nearest row. Files are vertical columns of squares, lettered *a* through *h*, beginning from White's left. Squares are named by combining the letter of the file with the number of the intersecting rank, as shown in diagram A. In diagram B, the original position at the start of a game, White's queen occupies d1 and Black's d8. Squares are always named from White's point of view.

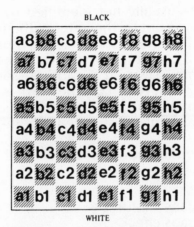

Diagram A: An algebraic grid

Diagram B: The starting position

The initials of the pieces are:

K for king
Q for queen
R for rook
B for bishop
N for knight

Pawns are usually not identified by initial when recording moves but by the letter of the file occupied. For example, a pawn on the b-file is a b-pawn. When a pawn makes a capture, only the two files are named. Thus, if a White pawn on f2 captures something (another pawn or a piece) on g3, the move is written fxg3. When indicating a capture, only the square on which the capture takes place is named, not the enemy unit captured.

You'll need to know these additional symbols:

x	means captures
+	means check
+ +	means checkmate
0-0	means castles kingside
0-0-0	means castles queenside
!	means good move
!!	means brilliant move
?	means questionable move
??	means blunder
?!	means risky move but worth considering
!?	means probably a good move but unclear
1.	means White's first move
1. . . .	means Black's first move (when appearing independently of White's)
2.	means White's second move
2. . . .	means Black's second move
3.	means White's third move (and so on)
(1-0)	means White wins
(0-1)	means Black wins

Using these symbols will enable you to follow sequences of chess moves without difficulty, assuming you first set up the diagram positions on a real chessboard. Consider diagram C, which contains a forced mate in three moves.

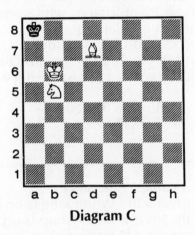

Diagram C

The winning variation is written like this: *1. Nc7+ Kb8 2. Na6+ Ka8 3. Bc6++ (1-0).*

1. Nc7+	means that White's first move is knight to c7 giving check
Kb8	means that Black's first move is king to b8
2. Na6+	means that White's second move is knight to a6 check
Ka8	means that Black's second move is king to a8
3. Bc6++	means that White's third move is bishop to c6 mate
(1-0)	means that White wins

Note that when a White move and a Black move are both given, the number of the move is given only once, just before White's move. The move number appears before a Black move when Black goes first or when the White move is absent due to a verbal or analytic comment. Also note that the moves actually played are given in boldface, while analyzed alternatives are given in regular type.

In *Chessercizes,* problem positions are given both in diagrams and in algebraic notation. Diagram C, for example, could be written the following way:

W: Kb6 Bd7 Nb5   (3)

B: Ka8   (1)

Where:

    W: means White pieces
    Kb6 means the White king is on b6
    Bd7 means a White bishop is on d7
    Nb5 means a White knight is on b5
    (3)   means White has 3 units
    B: means Black pieces
    Ka8 means the Black king is on a8
    (1)   means Black has one unit

When describing positions in algebraic notation, it is necessary to use the symbol "P" for pawn and "Ps" for pawns.

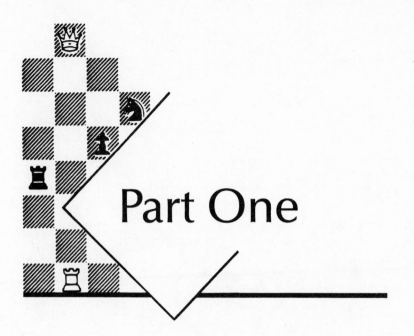

Part One

CHESSERCIZES
&
DIAGRAMS

1

MATING NETS

Players (White–Black)	Location
1. Burgess–Watson	Plymouth, Great Britain
2. Gheorghiu–Piket	Lugano, Switzerland
3. Sokolov–Miles	Biel, Switzerland
4. Psakhis–Tolnai	Dortmund, West Germany
5. Schroer–Kudrin	Bermuda
6. Sznapik–Schmidt	Slupsk, Poland
7. Kveinys–Tonchev	Starozagorski Bani, Bulgaria
8. Polgar–Hansen	Vetjstrup, Denmark
9. Nikolic–Hübner	Barcelona, Spain
10. Plachetka–Balashov	Trnava, Yugoslavia
11. Murey–Fedorowicz	Paris, France
12. Gelfand–Ftacnik	Debrecen, Hungary
13. Gauglitz–Sulava	Szeged, Hungary
14. Rohde–Shipman	New York, NY, USA

G. Burgess vs. W. Watson
PLYMOUTH, GREAT BRITAIN, 1989
BRITISH CHAMPIONSHIP

W: Kh2 Qc1 Rc3 Rg1 Bh1 Nf2 Ps a5 b4 d5 e4 f3 h3 (12)
B: Kh8 Qg5 Rd8 Rh7 Ne2 Nh4 Ps a6 b7 d6 e5 f4 (11)

MATING NET
Black to play and win

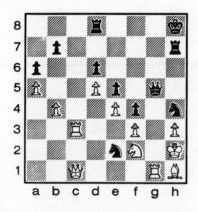

Beware of obvious moves that dissuade you from looking deeper. Black can easily end the attack on his queen either by capturing the g1-rook with his knight or by poising his knight on g3. He could even capture White's queen, 1. . . . Nxc1, but then Black's topples, 2. Rxg5.

If Black doesn't like any of that, he can mate in two moves, as in the actual game: **1. . . . Qg3 + !!** [*MATING NET*] **2. Rxg3 fxg3 mate (0-1)**.

2

W: Kb1 Qd8 Rd1 Ps b3 e4 f3 g4 h4   (8)
B: Kg7 Qe3 Rc4 Nf6 Ps a5 b4 e5 g6 h7   (9)

MATING NET
White to play and win

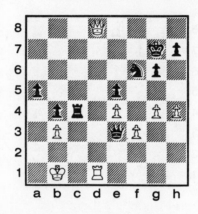

Poor Black! If only it were his turn, he could at least draw by perpetual check: Qxb3-a3-b3. But it's White's option and the situation uglifies, for Black's king is surrounded by White's queen-and-rook SWAT team.

It was all over after **1. Qe7+** [MATING NET] **1. . . . Kh6 2. Qf8** mate **(1-0).** Mate could be forestalled by 1. . . . Kg8, but it's still mate after 2. Rd8+ Ne8 3. Rxe8.

Another way to lose after 1. Qe7+ is 1. . . . Kh8 2. Rd8+ Ng8 3. Qf6 mate (or 3. Qxe5 mate).

I. SOKOLOV VS. A. MILES
BIEL, SWITZERLAND, 1989

W: Kg1 Qc6 Ra1 Rf1 Ba4 Ps a3 b2 c4 d5 e4 f4 g2 h4 (13)
B: Kd8 Qd2 Ra8 Rb8 Nf6 Ps a5 c7 c5 d6 e5 f7 g7 h7 (13)

MATING NET
Black to play and win

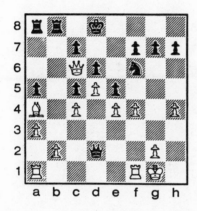

Appearances can be deceptive. White's queen and bishop look like a winning battery on the a4-e8 diagonal, though Black's knight guards against the mating threats at d7 and e8. Another bulwark is the b8-rook, which defends the a8-rook, attacked by White's queen.

Black pierced this blustery facade with **1. . . . Rxb2!** [*MATING NET*], abandoning his a8-rook and going for the gold at g2. After **2. Qxa8 + Ke7,** White gave up **(0-1)**, for his second rank is indefensible to Black's marauding queen and rook.

4

L. Psakhis vs. T. Tolnai
DORTMUND, WEST GERMANY, 1989

W: Kg3 Qa7 Rc3 Bg1 Ps a2 b4 c2 e4 h4   (9)
B: Kh7 Qc1 Re2 Ng4 Ps c6 e6 f7 g6 h5   (9)

MATING NET
Black to play and win

The cannon are loaded, but what of it? Black wins quickly by **1. . . . Qe1+** [*MATING NET*], forking king and rook. Since White's rook is a goner, he must get out of check by attacking Black's rook, **2. Kf3**, an eye for an eye.

There followed **2. . . . Qf1+ 3. Kg3,** and white resigned **(0-1)**. Black's two-gun salute (queen and rook) tells after 3. . . . Rg2+ 4. Kh3 Rxg1 discovered mate.

If Black missed that there was also 4. . . . Rh2+ 5. Kg3 Rh3 mate. One move longer, but just as deadly.

5

J. SCHROER VS. S. KUDRIN
BERMUDA, 1989
BERMUDA INTERNATIONAL

W: Kg3 Qb5 Ra1 Nc3 Ps a2 e4 g4 g2 h4   (9)
B: Kg8 Qd4 Be3 Nd2 Ps a7 b7 e7 g6 h7   (9)

MATING NET
Black to play and win

Black stands well with a queen and two pieces aimed at White's solitary king. But he still should exercise a bit of caution. If he takes the knight, 1. . . . Qxc3, then 2. Qe8+ draws. For example, after 2. . . . Kg7, 3. Qxe7+ Kg8 4. Qe8+ draws by repetition. If Black answers 3. Qxe7+ with 3. . . . Kh6, then 4. Qf8+ Qg7 5. g5+ (deflection) wins Black's queen. Even worse is 3. . . . Kh8, allowing 4. Qf8 mate.

The winning move was **1. . . . Bf4+!** [*MATING NET*], preventing White's king from scurrying back to h2 for shelter. After **2. Kxf4** (2. Kh3 is met by 2. . . . Qe3+ 3. g3 Qxg3 mate) **2. . . . Qf2+ 3. Ke5** (or 3. Kg5, allowing Black to mate with the queen at e3) **3. . . . Qf6+ 4. Kd5,** Black mated by **4. . . . Qd6++ (0-1)**.

6

A. Sznapik vs. W. Schmidt
SLUPSK, POLAND, 1989
POLISH CHAMPIONSHIP

W: Kf2 Qc5 Rc8 Ne2 Ps a3 b4 e5 f4 g2   (9)
B: Kd7 Qd1 Rh1 Rh2 Ps a6 b7 d5 e6 f7 g6   (10)

MATING NET
Black to play and win

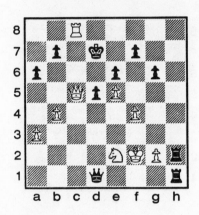

If only it were White's turn, he would simply move his queen to c7, where, supported by his rook, it would give checkmate. But this is air bubbles. It's Black's turn, and White's exposed kingside cannot be defended.

The last barrier is cleared away with **1. . . . Rxg2 +!** [*MATING NET*], which compels **2. Kxg2**, for 2. Ke3 comes to a bad end after the finalizing 2. . . . Qxe2 + 3. Kd4 Qd2 mate.

Black concluded his assault with **2. . . . Qf1 + 3. Kg3 Qh3 +**, and white resigned **(0-1)**. If White continues 4. Kf2, Black mates by 4. . . . Rf1.

A. Kveinys vs. M. Tonchev

STAROZAGORSKI BANI, BULGARIA, 1989

W: Kh1 Qh5 Rf1 Rh3 Nh6 Ps a2 c2 g2 h2   (9)
B: Kg7 Qb2 Ra8 Rf8 Bc8 Nh7 Ps a6 b7 e6 e4 g5   (11)

MATING NET
White to play and win

Underdog Black has yet to complete his development, and his queen is derelict on the queenside,
outside the main theater (as if it had rapaciously seized
a poison b-pawn). Meanwhile, White's pieces are ready
to strike on the kingside.

Raucous hurrahs after **1. Rf7 +** [*MATING NET*], and
Black resigned **(1-0)**, observing that he was trapped in a
forced mate.

White's invasion can be addressed in two ways:
the f7-rook can be captured or the king can scurry to
the corner. If 1. . . . Rxf7, White mates by 2. Qxf7 +
Kh8 3. Qg8 + + . The retreat 1. . . . Kh8 fares no better,
for 2. Rxh7 + ! Kxh7 3. Nf5 + Kg8 4. Qh7 is mate.

8

J. Polgar vs. L. B. Hansen
VETJSTRUP, DENMARK, 1989
POLITIKEN CUP

W: Kh4 Qh6 Rb7 Rf3 Bc5 Ps a4 d4 h3   (8)
B: Kg8 Qg2 Rd8 Re2 Nc6 Ps a7 d5 f7 g6   (9)

MATING NET
White to play and win

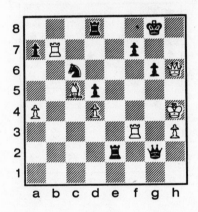

Of all White's various winning lines, none is so decisive, as immediate, and as brilliant as **1. Qg7+!!** [*MATING NET*], forcing Black's resignation **(1-0)**.

After 1. . . . Kxg7, White wins by 2. Rfxf7+ Kg8 (2. . . . Kh6 encounters 3. Rh7 mate) 3. Rg7+ Kh8 4. Rh7+ Kg8 5. Rbg7 mate.

9

P. Nikolic vs. R. Hübner

BARCELONA, SPAIN, 1989
WORLD CUP, ROUND 1

W: Kg1 Qe4 Rc4 Nc5 Ps b3 e7 f4 g2 h3   (9)
B: Kg8 Qd2 Rd8 Ne3 Ps a5 c7 f7 g7 h7   (9)

MATING NET
Black to play and win

    White's one pawn on the seventh rank issues two threats: to capture the rook at d8 and to promote to a queen or rook at e8, with mate to follow. These threats are empty, however, since it's Black's turn. He forces mate commencing with the intrusion **1. . . . Qe1+** [*MATING NET*].

    White had to reply 2. Kh2, but after **2. . . . Ng4+!** was forced to resign **(0-1)**. If the knight is taken, 3. hxg4, Black mates by 3. . . . Qh4+ 4. Kg1 Rd1+ 5. Qe1 Rxe1++.

J. Plachetka vs. Y. Balashov
TRNAVA, YUGOSLAVIA, 1989
"A" SECTION

W: Kh4 Rb7 Rf7 Ps d4 g4 (5)
B: Kg6 Ra4 Re3 Ps d5 h6 (5)

MATING NET
White to play and win

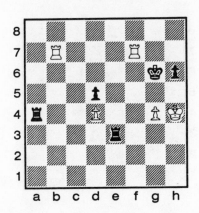

An even endgame, two rooks and two pawns each, but not quite equal. While White's king and rooks are coordinating beautifully, Black's pieces still need a few moves to sort things out.

White denied Black the chance with **1. Rg7 +**, which forced **1. . . . Kf6**. There followed **2. Rh7!**, threatening mate, which in turn was countered by **2. . . . Kg6**.

Black's attempt to supply his king with a temporary haven by playing 2. . . . Rxd4 fails to 3. Rxh6+ Ke5 4. Re7 + Kf4 5. Rf6 mate. Here Black's rooks actually interfere with their own king's escape.

The cordon was finally drawn around the Black king by **3. Rbf7!** [*MATING NET*], and Black deemed it prudent to resign **(1-0)**. Mate by Rh7-g7 can only be postponed, not averted. For example, if 3. . . . h5, then 4. Rhg7+ Kh6 5. g5+ + .

11

Y. MUREY VS. J. FEDOROWICZ
PARIS, FRANCE, 1989

W: Kh4 Qc6 Rb1 Rh1 Bf1 Nf3 Ps a2 b2 f4 g2 h3   (11)
B: Kg8 Qe3 Ra8 Rf8 Be6 Ps c4 g6 h7   (8)

MATING NET
Black to play and win

When a king stands on its fourth rank, exposed to attack from three enemy pieces, the end can't be far away. And it wasn't; the knell sounded with **1. ... Qf2+!** [*MATING NET*], convincing White to resign **(0-1)**.

Suppose White doesn't throw in the towel but plays 2. Kg5 instead? Then 2. . . . Rf5+ 3. Kh6 (or 3. Kg4 h5 mate) leads to 3. . . . Rh5 mate.

White can try to block the Black queen-check with 2. g3, but that is busted by 2. . . . Rxf4+ 3. Kg5 Qxg3+ 4. Kh6 Rh4+ 5. Nxh4 Qe3 mate (or 5. . . . Qf4 mate or 5. . . . Qxh4 mate).

12

B. GELFAND VS. L. FTACNIK

DEBRECEN, HUNGARY, 1989

W: Kh2 Rf1 Rg3 Bb2 Bg6 Ps a2 c4 d5 g2   (9)
B: Kg8 Qd6 Ra8 Bc8 Ps a7 b6 c5 h4   (8)

MATING NET
White to play and win

White's g3-rook is pinned by the queen and attacked by the h-pawn. So if White wanted to give a discovered check along the g-file that would save his rook from capture, it would have to be a double check. And so it was: **1. Bh7 +!** [*MATING NET*].

After the compulsory **1. . . . Kxh7,** White put the coda on his score with **2. Rf7 + Kh6 3. Bc1 +.** Mate only two moves away, Black resigned **(1-0).**

After 3. . . . Kh5, the game would have ended 4. Rh7 + Qh6 5. Rxh6 mate. And if Black jettisons his queen by 3. . . . Qf4, White still forces mate via 4. Bxf4 + Kh5 5. Rh7 + +.

13

G. Gauglitz vs. N. Sulava
SZEGED, HUNGARY, 1989

W: Kf1 Ra1 Rb7 Ba4 Ng1 Ps a2 b2 e4 g2   (9)
B: Kf8 Rd8 Rh1 Ne7 Ps a6 c3 e6 f7 g7 g3   (10)

MATING NET
Black to play and win

White has a lovely extra bishop, but his knight is pinned to his king and Black's rooks control important freeways of attack. This game bluntly ended with **1. . . . Rd2!** [*MATING NET*], setting up a devilish mating pattern with a rook check at f2 and then mate by capturing the knight.

The cost of Black's invasion was a few checks and the loss of the e7-knight by **2. Rb8+ Nc8 3. Rxc8+ Ke7.** If White's e-pawn were at e5 instead of e4, White had 4. Re8 mate.

But that was just a pipe dream. The actual game concluded **4. Rc7+ Kf6 5. e5+ Kg6,** and White resigned **(0-1)**. He had no satisfactory answer to the threat of Rd2-f2+.

14

M. ROHDE VS. W. SHIPMAN

NEW YORK, NY, USA, 1989
MANHATTAN CHESS CLUB CHAMPIONSHIP

W: Kg1 Qg5 Rg3 Bc4 Nd6 Ps a2 b2 e5 f2 g2 h3   (11)
B: Kd7 Qc7 Ra8 Rd8 Bc6 Nb7 Ps a7 b6 e6 f7   (10)

MATING NET
White to play and win

Though ahead by a rook, Black has no legal king move, in the face of White's pieces swarming with sudden-strike capability. White must act quickly to keep Black's king homeless.

The pre-emptor was **1. Bxe6 +!** [*MATING NET*]. Without a safe retreat, Black's king was forced to make do with **1. . . . Kxe6.** Prohibited was the alternative capture with the f-pawn, **1. . . . fxe6,** because of the silencer, **2. Qg7 mate.**

White followed with **2. Qf5 +**, driving the enemy king to the open center, **2. . . . Kd5**. Of course, 2. . . . Ke7 is met by 3. Qxf7 mate.

Play concluded **3. Rd3 + Kc5 4. e6 + Kb4 5. Rd4** mate *(1-0)*. Black can delay the result by answering 4. . . . Bd5, but mate still comes after 5. Qxd5 + Kb4 6. Qb5 + +.

2

MATING ATTACKS I

15

W: Kf3 Rd8 Rh8 Bg4 Ps a4 e3 g5   (7)
B: Kg6 Rc7 Rf7 Bb4 Ps a7 b6 f4 g7   (8)

MATING ATTACK
White to play and win

Both sides are flexing rook muscles. Black, more-over, has the chance to unveil a discovered check on the f-file. A comparison of the two kings, however, shows that while White's can be checked, Black's can be mated.

White has to avoid temptation, that's all. He could gain the exchange (a rook for a bishop) by 1. Bh5+, skewering the king and rook. That would leave Black some chances to resist. Remember Emanuel Lasker's maxim: If you see a good move, look for a better one! A move better than 1. Bh5+ is **1. Rd5!** [*MATING AT-*

TACK]. It guards the g-pawn and the escape square f5, setting up the threat of 2. Bh5 mate.

Black tried an obligatory check, **1. . . . fxe3 +**, but after **2. Kg3** resigned (**1-0**). With 2. . . . Be1 + 3. Kh3, the checks end along with Black's hope.

L. Ljubojevic vs. L. Portisch
LINARES, SPAIN, 1989
ROUND 7

W: Ka1 Rd1 Rf1 Nc3 Ne4 Ps a3 b2 d5 g4   (9)
B: Ke5 Rb8 Rb3 Be7 Na5 Ps a6 c4 g6   (8)

MATING ATTACK
White to play and win

Does Black have something? His rooks are doubled on the b-file and his bishop and knight are in range of the White king. The square b3 is particularly weak, Black owning it as a base of operations. On the other hand, it's White's turn, and his own attack slices deep to Black's solitary, centrally exposed king.

After **1. d6!**, Black resigned **(1-0)**. His bishop is menaced by White's d-pawn and his knight and king are set up for a rook-fork, Rd1-d5 +. Both the bishop and knight can be saved by retreating the bishop to d8, where it guards the a5-knight. But then 2. Rd5 + [*MATING ATTACK*] 2. . . . Ke6 3. Nc5 + + closes the final chapter.

V. ANAND VS. I. SOKOLOV
WIJK AAN ZEE, NETHERLANDS, 1989
ROUND 3

W: Kb1 Qb4 Rf1 Bh4 Nc5 Ps a2 b2 c2 e5 g4 h3   (11)
B: Ke8 Qh6 Ra8 Be6 Nb6 Ps a4 c7 c6 d5 g7 h7   (11)

MATING ATTACK
White to play and win

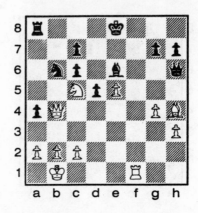

The White knight at c5 veils two lethal threats: mate at e7 and a winning check at f8. White could clear the a3-f8 diagonal, allowing the queen's entrance, by capturing on e6, but Black could cope by taking back with the queen.

The road to Mandalay is **1. Na6!** [*MATING AT-TACK*], opening the critical diagonal and additionally menacing a knight-fork at c7. To thwart the e7-mate, Black squashed White's bishop, **1. . . . Qxh4,** still leaving one White threat unanswered. Mate was the result of **2. Qf8+ Kd7 3. Nc5++.** In the end, the knight delivers the coup de grace by returning to its starting point.

M. Krasenkov vs. V. Arbakov
MOSCOW, USSR, 1989

W: Kg1 Qf4 Rb1 Bc5 Ps d4 e6 f3 g4 h2   (9)
B: Kc4 Qd5 Rc8 Bb7 Ps c7 c3   (6)

MATING ATTACK
White to play and win

Three pawns more for White than Black, though the opposite-color bishops reduce the importance of extra pawns. The critical issue, however, is Black's king trapped behind enemy lines with no immediate way out but kicking like a wounded dinosaur. Can it find an escape before being captured?

Pipe dream. The iron door clanged down with **1. Qe3!** [*MATING ATTACK*], setting up the final 2. Rb4 mate. No adequate reply in sight, Black resigned **(1-0)**.

Black can ward off mate by the sacrifice of his queen, 1. . . . Qxc5, but that leads to a hopeless, eventually losing game. The most plausible try is 1. . . . .

Qxf3, clearing d5 for the king's escape and threatening mate at g2. But this too fails as 2. Rb4+ Kd5 3. Qxf3+ wins the queen and more.

One more possibility, 1. . . . Qc6, flops after 2. Rb4+ Kd5 3. Qe4 mate (or 3. Qe5 mate).

19

A. KARPOV VS. V. SALOV
ROTTERDAM, NETHERLANDS, 1989
ROTTERDAM WORLD CUP, ROUND 15

W: Kg4 Rc3 Be5 Nc5 Ps f3 g3 (6)
B: Kg6 Qf1 Ps a5 d5 e6 h6 (6)

MATING ATTACK
Black to play and win

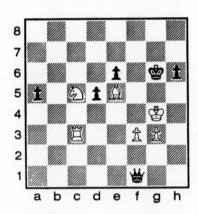

The forces: White has three pieces (rook, bishop, and knight) and Black has one (the queen). The pieces would be stronger if they worked together and supported each other as a team; the queen stands out because the three pieces are in disarray and scattered. Worsening White's situation is his vulnerable king at g4. Black's queen has plenty of targets.

Black found **1. . . . Qh1,** threatening 2. . . . Qh5 + 3. Kf4 Qg5 + + [*MATING ATTACK*]. White fled, **2. Kf4,** but after **2. . . . Qh5,** the mate threat was still on and White's bishop was in danger too.

The final moves were the desperate **3. Ke3 Qxe5+ 4. Kd2 d4,** and White surrendered **(0-1).** In order to break Black's offensive, White has to cede more material, losing even faster.

A. MILES VS. Y. GRUENFELD

NEW YORK, NY, USA, 1989
WORLD OPEN

W: Kb1 Qd6 Rd1 Ne6 Ps a2 b2 e7   (7)
B: Kh4 Qg2 Re8 Bc6 Ps a6 b7 f6 g7 h5   (9)

MATING ATTACK
White to play and win

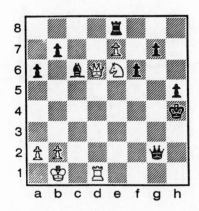

The attacking and defending proclivities of a king come forward in the endgame. But this is a middlegame, with unrestrained major pieces running wild, reducing Black's king at h4 to a sitting duck.

White cooked the kingly goose with **1. Qf4 +** [*MATING ATTACK*]. If Black answers 2. . . . Kh3, then 2. Rd3 + wins quickly.

Instead Black blocked the check, **1. . . . Qg4,** and after **2. Qh2 +** turned over his king **(1-0)**. If he had stayed to the finish, he would have witnessed 2. . . . Qh3 3. Rd4 + Be4 + 4. Rxe4 mate.

C. HOI VS. S. MOHR
GAUSDAL, NORWAY, 1989
GAUSDAL ARNOLD CUP

W: Kb1 Qb7 Rd1 Bc4 Ps a2 b3 c2 f2 g2   (9)
B: Kd6 Qd8 Ra8 Rf5 Ps a7 d4 e5   (7)

MATING ATTACK
White to play and win

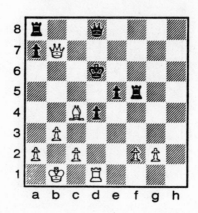

His king's retreat cut off and with almost no pawn cover, except in the center, Black is forced to run. Invasion beckons on the flank. The h-file is a suitable conduit, and White seizes it by **1. Rh1!** [*MATING AT-TACK*]. Black resigned (**1-0**).

White's threat: 2. Rh6+ Kc5 3. Qb5 mate or 3. Rc6 mate. Should Black choose to answer differently on his second move, he merely loses differently: 2. . . . Rf6 3. Rxf6+ Qxf6 4. Qxa8, putting White clearly ahead.

To avoid ignominious defeat, Black can try 1. . . . Rf6 (or even 1. . . . Qf8). But then 2. Rh7 menaces mate by 3. Qd5. If Black instead fashions an escape hatch for his king, 1. . . . e4, then he goes down anyway via 2. Rh6+ Ke5 3. Qg7+ Rf6 (if 3. . . . Kf4, then 4. Qg3 is mate) 4. Qg5+ gains the f6-rook, for 4. . . . Rf5 is bludgeoned by 5. Re6 mate. That's all, folks.

22

R. VAGANYAN VS. G. SAX

ROTTERDAM, NETHERLANDS, 1989
WORLD CUP, ROUND 7

W: Kf3 Qe1 Bf1 Nd2 Ps a2 d5 e4 f4 g5 g3   (10)
B: Kg8 Qg1 Rc8 Re8 Ps a6 d6 f7 g6 h7   (9)

MATING ATTACK
Black to play and win

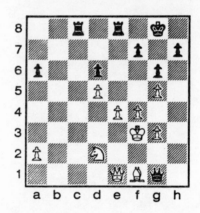

Two rooks for a bishop and knight puts Black ahead by two exchanges. White has only one extra pawn as material compensation. Furthermore, his king is vulnerable to attack.

Black wrapped up matters by **1. . . . Rc3 +**, forcing **2. Kg4**. The unpleasant follow-up was **2. . . . Qh1!** [*MATING ATTACK*]. White's only reasonable response to stop Qh5 was **3. f5**, which led to **3. . . . Qh5 + 4. Kf4 h6!**, and White resigned **(0-1)**.

On 5. gxh6, Black mates by 5. . . . g5 + +; and 5. Nf3 is mated by 5. . . . Rxf3 + + or 5. . . . Qxf3 + +. Meanwhile, Black threatens both h6xg5 mate and Qxg5 mate. Just too much for anyone to cope with.

23

A. Karpov vs. A. Yusupov

ROTTERDAM, NETHERLANDS, 1989
WORLD CUP TOURNAMENT, ROUND 11

W: Kg1 Qf3 Rf7 Ps a2 b3 f2 h3 (7)
B: Kb6 Qg5 Re5 Ps a5 g2 h5 (6)

MATING ATTACK
White to play and win

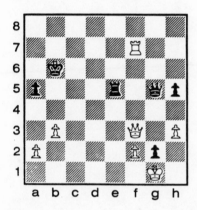

A tandem queen and rook can devastate an enemy king, especially on an open board. Both players in this attack are gifted with lethal force. Since both kings are vulnerable, it's a matter of who moves first. If it were Black's turn, 1. . . . Re1+ would force mate the next move.

But White slings the first stone. He forced Black into resigning after **1. Rb7+** [*MATING ATTACK*] **1. . . . Kc5** (if 1. . . . Ka6, then 2. Qc6++ is mate) **2. Rc7+ Kb4.**

On 2. . . . Kd6, White mates by 3. Qc6++. If

2. . . . Kb6, White mates by either 3. Qc6+ + or 3. Qb7+ +. And if 2. . . . Kd4, then 3. Rc4+ + is mate.

After 3. **Qf8+,** Black resigned **(1-0)**, for he loses material or gets mated. If 3. . . . Rc5, then 4. a3+ (deflection) forces the king to abandon the rook, for 4. . . . Kb5 is answered by 5. Qb8+ and mate next move. After 3. . . . Kb5, Black is mated by 4. Qb8+ Ka6 5. Qb7+ + or 5. Ra7+ +. For good measure, White has up his sleeve 3. . . . Kb5 4. a4+ followed by 5. Qd6 mate.

24

M. SION VS. Z. POLGAR
SALAMANCA, SPAIN, 1989

W: Ke4 Qd3 Bh3 Ps a4 b3 f4   (6)
B: Kg7 Qg1 Bh4 Ps a7 b6 f7 g6   (7)

MATING ATTACK
Black to play and win

White's lame king is a sitting duck in the center. Black defeathers it with **1. . . . f5 +** [*MATING ATTACK*] **2. Kd5.**

On 2. Kf3, Black mates with 2. . . . Qf2 + + ; if instead 2. Bxf5 gxf5 + 3. Kxf5, Black skewers the queen with 3. . . . Qg6 + ; or if 2. Ke5, then 2. . . . Qc5 + , when 3. Ke6 transposes into the main line, while 3. Qd5 loses to 3. . . . Bf6 + 4. Ke6 Qe7 mate.

The game terminated after **2. . . . Qc5 + 3. Ke6 Qc6 + 4. Qd6** (or 4. Ke5, which is rebuffed by 4. . . . Bf6 + + , a criss-cross mate) **4. . . . Qe8 + 5. Kd5 Qe4 mate (0-1).**

25

G. SAX VS. V. TSESHKOVSKY
WIJK AAN ZEE, NETHERLANDS, 1989
ROUND 8

W: Kd2 Rc7 Nc5 Ps a2 b3 f5 g2 h3   (8)
B: Kf8 Rd5 Nf7 Ps a6 b5 d4 h7   (7)

MATING ATTACK
White to play and win

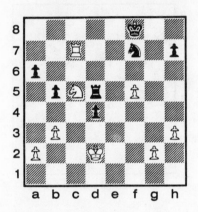

It appears that White has no real mating chances, since his pieces are not fully integrated. Yet the rook, knight and f5-pawn equal the value of a queen (9 points), which is a lethal weapon. The move igniting them into an effective force is **1. Ne6 +**.

Black has two options. He can obtain a losing game by moving his king back to the kingside, 1. . . . Kg8, but that drops a knight to 2. Rc8 +, when Black must sacrifice his knight to stop check and vacate f7 for his king.

The other possibility, **1. . . . Ke8**, the move chosen,

was countered by **2. f6!** [*MATING ATTACK*]. Delayed defeat is an agony, so Black resigned (**1-0**). Mate can be stopped by 2. . . . Rd7, but 3. Rc8+ Nd8 4. Rxd8+ (or 4. Nxd8) 4. . . . Rxd8 5. f7+ Kxf7 6. Nxd8+ still wins for White.

26

S. Marjanovic vs. D. Sermek
BLED, YUGOSLAVIA, 1989

W: Kf1 Qb5 Ra6 Rd1 Nb1 Ps b6 b2 c3 e4 f2 g3   (11)
B: Kf8 Qh5 Rd8 Rh8 Nf5 Ps c7 d6 e5 f7 g7 g4   (11)

MATING ATTACK
Black to play and win

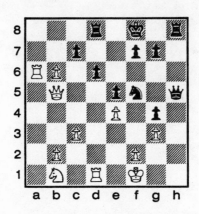

White is gung-ho on the queenside, but Black eyes bigger game on the kingside. But how should he work it? If the Black queen checks at h1, the White king scurries away via the second rank. To stop this escape, Black strips away the enemy pawn cover: **1. . . . Nxg3 + !** [MATING ATTACK].

If White takes the knight, 2. fxg3, Black crowns his play by 2. . . . Qh1 + 3. Ke2 Rh2 + (taking advantage of the cleared second rank) 4. Kd3 (4. Ke3 Qf3 is mate) Qxd1 + 5. Kc4 Qf1 + 6. Kb3 (6. Kb4 is dismissed by 6. . . . Rxb2 +, skewering the queen) 6. . . . Qxb5 +, winning the queen and more.

Naturally, White declined the offer of the knight, sidestepping with **2. Ke1**, hoping for a haven on the queenside through d2. Black thwarted this by **2. . . . Qg5!**, guarding d2 and readying Rh1 mate.

Since 3. fxg3 quickly falls to 3. . . . Qe3+ 4. Kf1 Rh1+ 5. Kg2 Qf3 mate, White resigned **(0-1)**.

27

W: Kg1 Qd7 Rb7 Ps a2 d3 f2 g3 h2   (8)
B: Kg6 Qe5 Rh8 Ps a7 d4 f5 g7 h7   (8)

MATING ATTACK
White to play and win

White's doubled major pieces on the seventh rank are an irresistible force and Black's king is not an invincible object. Fortunes are clarified by **1. Qf7+** [*MATING ATTACK*]. After **1. ... Kh6,** White toppled the throne with **2. Re7 (1-0).**

Black must lose at least a rook. If 2. ... Qc5, to keep watch over White's rook, White forges through with 3. Qxg7+ Kh5 4. Re6, threatening 5. Rh6 mate.

Black has a spite check, 4. ... Qc1+, but after 5. Kg2, he has no way to save the rook without being mated. If Black continues, for example, 5. ... Rc8, then 6. Qxh7+ Kg4 (or 6. ... Kg5 7. Qh4 mate) 7. Qh4 mates.

A. CHERNIN VS. U. BONSCH
LUGANO, SWITZERLAND, 1989

W: Kh3 Qg5 Re1 Re5 Nf1 Ps a4 b5 f4 g3 h2   (10)
B: Kg8 Qf7 Rc2 Rf2 Nf8 Ps a7 b6 g7 h5   (9)

MATING ATTACK
Black to play and win

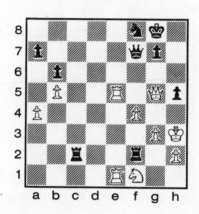

    Doubled rooks on the seventh rank seems advantageous to Black, but the point of attack, h2, is twice guarded. The solution? Give a triple attack. This Black did by **1. . . . Qa2!** [*MATING ATTACK*], tripling major pieces on Black's seventh rank and threatening 2. . . . Rxh2+ 3. Nxh2 Rxh2 mate.

    White tried a getaway by **2. g4,** which should have lost at once to 2. . . . Rf3+ 3. Kh4 (if 3. Ng3, then 3. . . . Rxh2++ is mate) 3. . . . Rxh2+ 4. Nxh2 Qxh2 mate.

    Black missed this possibility, but found **2. . . . Rxh2+ 3. Kg3 Rcg2+ 4. Kf3 Qf2+,** compelling White's resignation **(0-1).** If Black hadn't found *4. . . . Qf2+,* there was always 4. . . . Rh3+ 5. Ke4 Qc2+ 6. Kd5 Rd3+ and mate in two moves.

29

M. Chiburdanidze vs. H. Hoffman

LUGANO, SWITZERLAND, 1989

W: Kg1 Qc3 Rc1 Rd4 Bf4 Bg2 Ps b2 d6 f2 g3 h2 (11)
B: Kd8 Qb6 Rb8 Rh8 Bf8 Nd7 Ne8 Ps a6 f7 g7 h6 (11)

MATING ATTACK
White to play and win

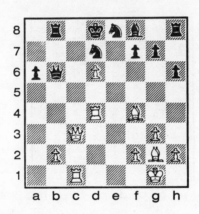

The scales seem balanced. Two knights for a bishop and pawn: material edge to Black. But the extra pawn at d6 confers the tactical edge on White.

Suddenly the scales became unbalanced by **1. Qc7+!!**. Play proceeded **1. ... Nxc7 2. dxc7+ Ke8** (or 2. ... Ke7, when White interpolates 3. Rxd7+ and follows with 4. cxb8/Q) **3. Re4+** [*MATING ATTACK*] **3. ... Be7 4. cxb8/Q+ Nxb8 5. Rc8+ Kd7.** Here White introduced **6. Bh3+**, and Black surrendered (**1-0**).

If Black continues 6. ... Qe6, he loses to 7. Bxe6+ fxe6 8. Rxh8, with White having two rooks more than Black. If Black blunders, 6. ... f5, then 7. Bxf5+ Qe6 8. Bxe6++.

30

Y. Seirawan vs. A. Karpov

ROTTERDAM, NETHERLANDS, 1989
WORLD CUP, ROUND 3

W: Ke1 Qa7 Rc1 Nd4 Ps a3 b2 e3 g3   (8)
B: Kg8 Qf6 Rd8 Bg4 Ps b6 f7 g7 h5   (8)

MATING ATTACK
Black to play and win

White's king is in a pickle, brined by Black's queen, rook, and bishop. Two things immediately stand in Black's way: the knight at d4 and the pawn at e3. Both were belted with the shot, **1. . . . Rxd4!.** After **2. exd4 Qe6+** [*MATING ATTACK*], White's king was in real trouble.

White continued **3. Kd2,** for either 3. Kf1 or 3. Kf2 drops the rook to 3. . . . Qe2+ 4. Kg1 Qe3+ (of course, 5. Kf1 Bh3 is mate).

There followed **3. . . . Qe2+ 4. Kc3 Qe3+** (attacking the rook) **5. Kc2 Bf5+ 6. Kd1 Qxd4+ 7. Ke1** (7. Ke2

Qd3+ 8. Ke1 transposes back to the main variation) **7.
. . . Qe3+ 8. Kd1 Qd3+ 9. Ke1 Qxg3+ 10. Kd1** (10. Kf1
allows 10. . . . Bd3 mate) **10. . . . Qg1+ 11. Kd2 Qf2+**,
and White resigned **(0-1)**.

After 12. Kd1, Black mates by 12. . . . Bg4++,
while 12. Kc3 Qe3+ gains the rook.

3

MATING ATTACKS II

Players (White–Black)	Location
31. Luther–Judasin	Budapest, Hungary
32. Kamsky–Leveille	Buffalo, NY, USA
33. Smyslov–Chandler	Hastings, England
34. Vilela–Vera	Bayamo, Cuba
35. Adams–Spassky	Cannes, France
36. Gelfand–Benjamin	New York, NY, USA
37. Illescas–Kasparov	Barcelona, Spain
38. Sakaev–Komarov	USSR
39. Polgar–Suba	Rome, Italy
40. Sieglen–Wessein	West Germany
41. Miles–Hennigan	New York, NY, USA
42. Hjartarson–Karpov	Seattle, WA, USA
43. Miles–Alburt	Philadelphia, USA
44. Shirazi–Ivanov	Philadelphia, USA
45. Hübner–Hess	Lugano, Switzerland
46. Ehlvest–Salov	Rotterdam, Netherlands
47. Campora–Dreev	Moscow, USSR

31

T. LUTHER VS. L. JUDASIN
BUDAPEST, HUNGARY, 1989
BUDAPEST OPEN

W: Ka1 Qe6 Re2 Nb1 Nd2 Ps a2 a3 g4 h2   (9)
B: Kh8 Qd1 Rc1 Be7 Nf6 Ps b4 g7 h7   (8)

MATING ATTACK
Black to play and win

White is in trouble. His knights are immobilized, his rook is lashed to the defense of the d2-knight, and his king's position is exposed, particularly along the a1-h8 diagonal. White's only hope is the threat to Black's bishop and the somewhat fanciful notion of a back-rank mate.

Black combined defense and attack with **1. . . . Ng8!**, guarding the bishop, shielding the king, and preparing a bishop check at f6 [*MATING ATTACK*]. White's fancy evaporated, and with no adequate answers, he resigned (**0-1**).

Obviously, 2. g5 Bxg5 only delays the inevitable. Would 2. Re3 save the day? It blocks the a1-h8 diagonal all right, but also allows 2. . . . Qxd2, losing a knight. If White tries to flee, 2. Kb2, it's mate anyway by 2. . . . Qc2+ 3. Ka1 Qc3+ +.

32

G. KAMSKY VS. F. LEVEILLE

BUFFALO, NY, USA, 1989
CONTINENTAL OPEN

W: Kg1 Qg5 Rf2 Rf1 Ps a2 e5 g2   (7)
B: Kg8 Qd8 Rd6 Rd4 Ps a7 c3 d3 e6 f7 g6   (10)

MATING ATTACK
White to play and win

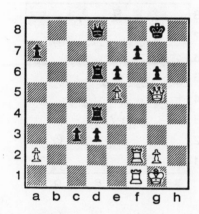

What's happening with the pawn attack on Black's
d6-rook? Nothing, because White's queen is hanging
to Black's. If White saves himself by a queen exchange,
Black in turn salvages his d6-rook by taking back on d8.
Thereafter his passed c- and d-pawns would be a real
science fiction menace.

Material considerations were circumvented by
1. Rxf7! [*MATING ATTACK*], and Black had to resign
(1-0). For example, if 1. . . . Qxg5, then 2. Rf8+ Kg7 (or
2. . . . Kh7) 3. R1f7+ Kh6 4. Rh8 is mate. With White's
queen ready to capture on g6, resignation was the
most reasonable course.

33

V. SMYSLOV VS. M. CHANDLER
HASTINGS, ENGLAND, 1989

W: Kh1 Qd3 Re5 Re1 Bg2 Ps a4 d5 g3 h4   (9)
B: Kh8 Qc5 Rc8 Rd8 Bb7 Ps a5 b6 g7 h6   (9)

MATING ATTACK
White to play and win

White has the lead in space, this game's final frontier. His pieces are primed for kingside excursions while Black's are earthbound on the queenside. In fact, White's d-pawn seems to divide the universe in half.

White jumped to hyperspace with **1. Qg6!**, a powerful invasion into the light-square hole, g6. Threat: 2. Re7 [*MATING ATTACK*].

Anticipating that assault, Black defended the g-pawn by **1. . . . Rg8.** He might have tried 1. . . . Qf8 instead, but 2. Re7 Ba8 3. Rf7 Qg8 4. Re7, tripling on the pitiless g-pawn, would win anyway.

A sidebar. After 1. Qg6!, it's a mistake to capture

on d5, 1. . . . Bxd5, for 2. Bxd5 Rxd5 3. Re8+ forces Black to stop mate by blocking with his queen, which loses the queen for a rook.

In the actual game, White answered Black's rook move to g8 by **2. Be4,** threatening 3. Qh7 mate. Black resigned (**1-0**), for his king can neither hide nor flee.

34

J. VILELA VS. R. VERA
BAYAMO, CUBA, 1989
10TH ANNUAL CARLOS DE CESPEDES MEMORIAL

W: Kc1 Qe3 Rd1 Rd2 Be5 Ps a2 b2 f2 g2 h2   (10)
B: Kg8 Qd8 Ra8 Rd7 Bf5 Ps a6 b7 c6 g7 h7   (10)

MATING ATTACK
White to play and win

The same number and kinds of pieces occupy time and space for both sides, except that White has a dark-square bishop and Black a light-square one. Since it's the middlegame, and opposite-color bishops give the attacker in effect an extra attacking piece, White has the advantage.

White started out by trading rooks, **1. Rxd7 Bxd7.** This left f7 more vulnerable, no longer guarded by the d7-rook. White then attacked along the weakened diagonal, a2-g8, **2. Qb3 +** [*MATING ATTACK*]. Convinced the board offered no hope, Black resigned **(1-0).**

If 2. . . . Kf8, to get out of check, then 3. Bd6 + Ke8 4. Qg8 is mate. Moving the king to the corner doesn't help, for 2. . . . Kh8 is met by 3. Qf7, promising g7-mate or gain of the d7-bishop. Black might try getting out of the d-file pin with the apparent time-gainer, 3. . . . Qg5 + , but 4. f4 would then cool his heels.

35

M. Adams vs. B. Spassky
CANNES, FRANCE, 1989
TOURNAMENT OF GENERATIONS

W: Kh1 Qg1 Rd1 Bd3 Nc5 Nf8 Ps a2 c3 d5 g2 h3   (11)
B: Kg8 Qh4 Rf2 Bc8 Nd6 Ps a6 b5 g6 h7   (9)

MATING ATTACK
Black to play and win

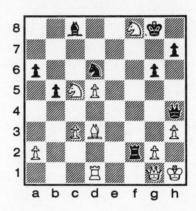

Black could capture on f8 and settle for being a pawn down. Or perhaps he should play for bigger game, since White's king is suffocating in the corner. (Besides, the f8-knight isn't going anywhere.)

With **1. . . . Bxh3** [*MATING ATTACK*], Black's goal verged on fruition, for he then threatened 2. . . . Bxg2! mate. And taking the bishop, 2. gxh3, doesn't save White, for 2. . . . Qxh3+ 3. Qh2 Qxh2++ is definitely mate.

White can try to break Black's attack by ditching his own precious queen for a rook and a bishop, 2. Qxf2 Qxf2 3. gxh3, but 3. . . . Qf3+, forking king and rook, unbalances the equation.

White decided on **2. Qh2,** preventing a discovered check along the h-file, but **2. . . . Rxg2 3. Qxd6 Rxa2** compelled White's resignation **(0-1)**. He was helpless against the looming discovered check on the h-file.

36

W: Ka2 Qb2 Re2 Ps a3 b3 c4 d5 e4 f5   (9)

B: Kf8 Qh3 Rc3 Ps a5 b6 c7 d6 e5 f7   (9)

MATING ATTACK
Black to play and win

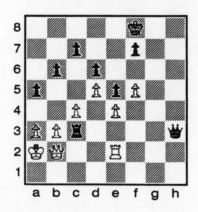

The White queen and rook line up defensively while their Black counterparts stand together offensively—a significant difference. White could play Rh2 if it weren't Black's move.

Black broke White's fragile queenside with **1. . . . a4!.** White doggedly ventured **2. bxa4,** but **2. . . . Qd3!** [*MATING ATTACK*], exploiting the weakened c-pawn, convinced him to resign (**0-1**).

If 3. Qd2, then 3. . . . Rxa3+ 4. Kb2 Qb3+ 5. Kc1 Ra1 mate. On 3. Re1, Black pins the queen by 3. . . . Rc2. Finally, if White essays 3. Rh2, hoping for counterplay, Black gains the White queen by 3. . . . Qxc4+ 4. Ka1 (if 4. Kb1, then 4. . . . Rb3) 4. . . . Rc1+.

37

M. ILLESCAS VS. G. KASPAROV

BARCELONA, SPAIN, 1989
WORLD CUP, ROUND 16

W: Kh1 Rh4 Pa3   (3)
B: Kf3 Rg5 Bh3   (3)

MATING ATTACK
Black to play and win

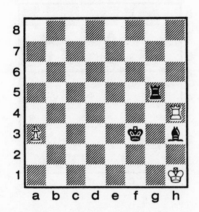

The endgame of king, rook and bishop against king, rook and pawn is usually drawn. One exception is when the side with the bishop can corner the enemy king. If the attacker's pieces are poised, mate or win of the opposing rook could ensue.

White resigned (**0-1**) after **1. . . . Kg3.** If 2. Rh8, then 2. . . . Re5 (threatening mate at e1) 3. Rg8+ Bg4 [*MATING ATTACK*] compels White to pitch his rook to delay mate.

And if 2. Rb4, for example, then 2. . . . Bg2+ 3. Kg1 Rh5 (threatening mate at h1) 4. Rb3+ Bf3 again forces the rook sacrifice.

38

SAKAEV VS. KOMAROV
USSR, 1989

W: Kh2 Qg4 Rc8 Rg1 Bf4 Bg2 Ps d5 e4 g3 h3   (10)
B: Kg7 Qa2 Rb2 Re7 Bd4 Nd7 Ps d6 f6 g6   (9)

MATING ATTACK
White to play and win

A double-barreled threat from Black: to take the rook at g1 with check and then to capture the g2-bishop. But White's muskets are also loaded, and aimed at the targets h8 (for his queen and rook to score a bulls-eye) and h6 (for his queen and bishop).

White played **1. Qh4!** [MATING ATTACK], allowing **1. . . . Bxg1 +**. After the back-step *2. Kh1* (White avoids 2. Kxg1 Rxg2 +) Black resigned (**1-0**), for he had no acceptable replies to the ominous checks at h8 and h6.

Say, for example, Black takes the bishop, 2. . . . Rxg2; then White wins by 3. Qh8 + Kf7 4. Qh7 mate (or 4. Qg8 mate).

Or if Black poses 2. . . . Nf8, temporarily blocking out the rook, then 3. Qh6+ followed by 4. Rxf8 mate. And if 2. . . . g5, obstructing the f4-bishop, then 3. Qh8+ Kg6 4. Rg8+ mates next move.

39

S. POLGAR VS. M. SUBA
ROME, ITALY, 1989

W: Kh1 Qh4 Re1 Rf1 Bh6 Ps a3 c4 d5 f6 g2 h2   (11)
B: Kh8 Qc5 Rc8 Re8 Bd7 Ps a6 a4 e5 f7 g6 h7   (11)

MATING ATTACK
White to play and win

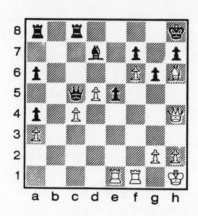

Black's forces are shifted to the queenside, leaving his king alone on the kingside. If he could simplify to an endgame, the bishops of opposite colors would increase the likelihood of a draw. But before the endgame, Dr. Siegbert Tarrasch once remarked, the gods have placed the middlegame.

White played **1. Re4** [MATING ATTACK], threatening 2. Bg7+ Kg8 3. Qxh7+ Kxh7 4. Rh4+ Kg8 5. Rh8 mate. Black defended with **1. ... Kg8,** then resigned **(1-0)** after **2. Bg7.** Mate could not be staved off.

If Black tries defending with 2. . . . h5, White answers 3. Qg5. From g5, White's queen threatens to zig to h6 and zag to h8 for mate. Hapless Black is helpless to stop this.

40

J. Sieglen vs. K. Wessein

WEST GERMANY, 1989
WEST GERMANY LEAGUE

W: Kh1 Qc1 Re3 Bf1 Nf5 Ps a2 b3 c6 e4 g3 h2   (11)
B: Kg7 Qh5 Rf8 Be6 Ng5 Ps a7 c7 e5 f2 g4   (10)

MATING ATTACK
Black to play and win

White has problems, such as the weakness of his
king's position, especially the light squares. Then
there's the plaguing presence of the Black f2-pawn,
which oversees g1 and ever threatens to promote.

Black must first divert the White e-pawn from the
a8-h1 diagonal, which he does by **1. ... Rxf5!**. After
2. exf5, Black exploits that diagonal by **2. ... Bd5 +.**

White blocked this check, *3. Bg2,* but that gnarled
the bishop in a pin. Black piled up on the pinned
piece, **3. ... Qh3!.** If White captures on d5, 4. Bxd5,

then Black promotes, 4. . . . f1/Q+, supported by the
h3-queen.

So White clogged the diagonal, **4. Rf3,** and resigned **(0-1)** after **4. . . . Nxf3 5. Bxh3 Ne1+!** (mating
net), before the obvious mate next move.

41

A. MILES VS. M. HENNIGAN

W: Kg1 Qg5 Rd1 Ra1 Bc4 Bh6 Ps a2 b2 c2 f2 g2 h2 (12)
B: Kg8 Qf5 Ra8 Re8 Bb7 Nb8 Ps a7 b6 c5 e5 f7 g6 h7 (13)

MATING ATTACK
White to play and win

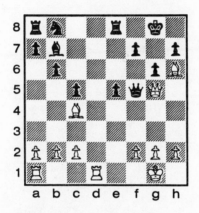

Black is one pawn richer than White, but he's not completely developed and his kingside dark squares are exposed to the enemy's wrath. White's queen and dark-square bishop are hulking. Moreover, White's light-square bishop threatens f7, pinning the f7-pawn, while a hefty White rook dominates the d-file unopposed. How does he integrate these disparate elements into a win?

The synergistic solution is **1. Qe7!**. The queen is immune to capture because of 2. Rd8 + and mate next move [*MATING ATTACK*]. Since White also confronts Black's b7-bishop, it was evacuated, **1. . . . Bc6.**

White then invaded, **2. Rd8,** and after **2. . . . Na6 3. Rxa8 Rxa8,** showed Black's futility by **4. Rd1!.** With no satisfactory defense to the pending check at d8 (on **4. . . . Qc8** White scores by **5. Qxf7+** or **5. Bxf7+**, followed by immediate mate), Black resigned (**1-0**).

42

W: Kh1 Qc2 Bb2 Bf1 Nb3 Nd1 Ps a3 f3 g2 h4   (10)
B: Kg8 Qe6 Ra8 Bb7 Bh2 Ng4 Ps c5 f7 g7 h6   (10)

MATING ATTACK
Black to play and win

It's bad for White, bad enough that he has only a knight for a rook. His kingside is also in danger, with holes and weaknesses on the dark squares and undefended units ready for tactical exploitation.

Black capitalized by **1. . . . Qe1!,** forking the f1-bishop and the h-pawn. Seeing no hope, White resigned **(0-1)**.

But suppose White captures the Black knight on g4. If 2. fxg4, Black replies 2. . . . Qxh4 [*MATING ATTACK*], with 3. . . . Bg3+ and 4. . . . Qh2 mate to follow.

Instead of capturing the g4-knight, if White guards

the f1-bishop, 2. Qc4, then Black has the convincing 2. . . . Bf4! (not 2. . . . Qxh4 because of 3. Qxg4). If White then captures the bishop, 3. Qxf4, Black's queen mates by taking the f1-bishop. If White takes the knight, 3. fxg4, he is mated by 3. . . . Qxh4+ 4. Kg1 Bh2+ 5. Kh1 Bg3+ 6. Kg1 Qh2++.

43

T. Miles vs. L. Alburt

PHILADELPHIA, PA, USA, 1989
WORLD OPEN, ROUND 7

W: Kg1 Qh5 Re2 Bb2 Nc3 Ps a2 b3 b5 d4 g2 h3   (11)
B: Kg8 Qg3 Rf8 Bb7 Nd7 Ps a7 c5 e6 g7   (9)

MATING ATTACK
Black to play and win

A wild one. White is two pawns to the good, but Black has the move and a powerful assault force: an entrenched queen, an unimpeded rook, and a sniping bishop. Matters were concluded with **1. . . . Bf3!** (fork), attacking White's queen and rook.

To save the queen, White had to play **2. Ne4,** swatting at Black's lady. But after **2. . . . Bxe4 3. Rxe4 Rf2** [*MATING ATTACK*], the battle has been lost and won.

White resigned (**0-1**) after **4. Qe8+ Nf8.** If 5. Rg4, then 5. . . . Rxg2+ 6. Kf1 Qf2 mate; or 6. Kh1 Qh2 mate, or 6. . . . Qxh3 mate, or 6. . . . Rh2 mate.

44

K. SHIRAZI VS. I. IVANOV

PHILADELPHIA, PA, USA, 1989
WORLD OPEN, ROUND 6

W: Kg1 Qb1 Ra7 Rd5 Ps a3 b4 e4 f2 g3 h2   (10)
B: Kf8 Qc4 Rc8 Bd4 Ne6 Ps b6 e5 f7 g6 h7   (10)

MATING ATTACK
Black to play and win

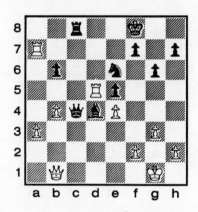

Though material is nominally even—bishop and knight for rook and pawn—Black's two minor pieces constitute a greater attacking potential. Also bad for White, his kingside is denuded of defenders.

Black struck suddenly with **1. . . . Qe2** [*MATING ATTACK*], and White resigned (**0-1**), having no satisfactory defense of f2. If White defends with 2. Qf1, then 2. . . . Rc1 (pin) forces mate: 3. Qxc1 Qxf2+ 4. Kh1 Qf3++.

White also goes down to mate after 2. Kg2 Qxf2+ 3. Kh3 Ng5+ 4. Kh4 (or 4. Kg4 Qf3+ 5. Kxg5 Be3+

— 86 —

6. Kh4 Qh5 mate) 4. . . . Nf3 + 5. Kg4 (or 5. Kh3 Qxh2 +
6. Kg4 Qh5 mate) 5. . . . h5 + 6. Kh3 Qxh2 mate.
 Equally hopeless is 2. Rxd4 Nxd4, when Black is up
a knight and verges on gaining more.

45

R. HÜBNER VS. R. HESS
LUGANO, SWITZERLAND, 1989
ROUND 1

W: Kg1 Qe3 Rf2 Rf1 Ne5 Ps a2 b4 c3 d4 g2 h2   (11)
B: Kc8 Qh6 Rf8 Rh8 Be6 Ps a6 b7 c6 c7 g5 h5   (11)

MATING ATTACK
White to play and win

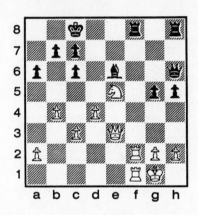

When kings are castled on opposite sides, the skirmish often hinges on which side's attack is more immediate. White, with the move, broke through with the pawn sacrifice, **1. d5!** [*MATING ATTACK*].

Taking the pawn with the bishop 1. . . . Bxd5, loses to the invasion 2. Qa7. A possible continuation might be 2. . . . Kd8 3. Qb8+ Ke7 4. Qxc7+ Ke6 5. Qd7+ Kxe5 6. Re2+ Be4 7. Rxe4+ (or 7. Qd4+ Ke6 8. Rxe4 mate) 7. . . . Kxe4 8. Qd4 mate.

So Black played **1. . . . Rxf2**, and after **2. Rxf2**, captured the d-pawn, **2. . . . cxd5.** Here he shied away from 2. . . . Bxd5 3. Qa7 Kd8 4. Qb8+ Ke7 5. Qxc7+

Ke6 6. Nf7 (fork), when neither of the double threats of 7. Qd6 mate and 7. Nxh6 could be neutralized. If, for example, 6. . . . Qf8, then 7. Nxg5 is mate anyway. White pursued with **3. Qa7,** and Black tried to clear out some debris with **3. . . . c6.** If 3. . . . Kd8, then 4. Qb8+ Ke7 5. Qxc7+ Ke8 6. Rf7! Bxf7 7. Qxf7+ Kd8 8. Qd7 is mate. After **4. Nf7,** Black resigned (**1-0**), having no better answer than 4. . . . Bxf7 5. Rxf7, White's insuperable threats looming over the seventh rank.

46

J. EHLVEST VS. V. SALOV
ROTTERDAM, NETHERLANDS, 1989
WORLD CUP, ROUND 16

W: Kg1 Qd4 Rd7 Rg5 Bf1 Ps a2 b2 c4 f3 g2   (10)
B: Kh8 Qe1 Rf8 Rf6 Ne3 Ps a6 b4 c6 f4   (9)

MATING ATTACK
White to play and win

Threats are flying on both directions here, but Black's king is somewhat more exposed and White's rooks have the edge—the f6-rook, in fact, pinned by White's queen. Meanwhile, White must contend with Black's aim to capture the bishop.

Surprisingly, he ignored that threat for the powerful centralization **1. Qe5!** (he could have protected the bishop by 1. Qd3). From e5, the queen radiates across the fifth rank and along the e-file, prepared with unanswerable threats.

In the game, after **1. ... Qxf1+ 2. Kh2 Qb1** (to

defend h7 and g6) **3. Rh5+ Kg8 4. Qe7** [*MATING AT-TACK*], Black resigned (**1-0**).

Can Black save his king? If 4. . . . Qg6, to guard g7, 5. Rg5 pins the queen and wins, for capturing the rook allows mate at h7. If instead 4. . . . R6f7, then 5. Qg5+ mates in two moves. Nor is 4. . . . R8f7 much better, for 5.Qe8+ Rf8 (5. . . . Kg7 6. Qh8+ Kg6 7. Qh6 mate is not very good either) 6. Rg5+, and it's mate in three more moves.

47

D. CAMPORA VS. A. DREEV
MOSCOW, USSR, 1989
REGIONAL A TOURNAMENT

W: Kg1 Qe2 Ra1 Re1 Bg5 Ps a3 b3 g3 h2   (9)
B: Kg8 Qc7 Rd8 Rf8 Bd5 Ps b5 e5 g7   (8)

MATING ATTACK
Black to play and win

The dark-square bishop is going at Black's d8-rook, but Black's light-square counterpart attacks key squares near the White king. If only Black's queen could reach h1, backed up by the bishop.

That goal in sight, Black brought the bishop all the way back, **1. . . . Ba8!!,** threatening Qb7-h1 [*MATING ATTACK*]. White tried **2. Qxb5,** fearing 2. Bxd8 Qc5 + 3. Qe3 Qd5 4. Qe4 Qxd8 5. Qxe5 Qb6 + 6. Re3 Qb7 7. Qe6 + Rf7 8. Qe8 + Kh7, when he must surrender a rook to avert mate.

In the game, Black aimed at White's queen, **2. . . .**

Rb8, and White resigned (**0-1**). He can stave off mate temporarily by 3. Qc4+ Qxc4 4. bxc4, but 4. . . . Rb2 sets up the threat to check on g2, followed by capturing on g3, giving discovered mate. Futility.

4

FORKS AND DOUBLE ATTACKS

Players (White–Black)	Location
48. Kasparov–Salov	Barcelona, Spain
49. Lanka–Glek	Moscow, USSR
50. Belyavsky–Kasparov	Barcelona, Spain
51. Salov–Short	Barcelona, Spain
52. Maus–Kinderman	Bad Worishofen, West Germany
53. Van der Weil–Sokolov	Haninge, Sweden
54. Kotronias–Goldin	Moscow, USSR
55. Ivanchuk–Torre	Biel, Switzerland
56. Ljubojevic–Speelman	Barcelona, Spain
57. Prie–Psakhis	Paris, France
58. Ehlvest–Fedorowicz	New York, USA
59. Belyavsky–Karpov	Linares, Spain

48

G. KASPAROV VS. V. SALOV

BARCELONA, SPAIN, 1989
WORLD CUP, ROUND 12

W: Kg1 Qc7 Rc1 Re1 Ps a2 b3 f2 g3 h2   (9)
B: Ke8 Qd7 Rf8 Bb7 Be7 Ps a6 d6 g6 h7   (9)

FORK
White to play and win

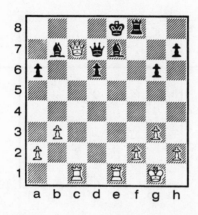

Easy figuring counts Black ahead, with two bishops for a rook and pawn. But it's White's turn, and he can force a win: **1. Qb8+ Kf7 2. Rc7** [*FORK*]. In the actual game, Black gave up (**1-0**), having few options.

If he continues 2. . . . Rxb8, then 3. Rxd7 forks the two bishops and insures the capture of one of them because of the pinned bishop at e7. White then comes out an exchange ahead. And if Black moves his queen out of attack, say to f5, then 3. Rexe7+ is decisive.

49

Z. LANKA VS. I. GLEK
MOSCOW, USSR, 1989
GMA TOURNAMENT

W: Kg1 Re1 Ba5 Ps a4 b5 c3   (6)
B: Kg4 Rf6 Be4 Ps b6 g2   (5)

DOUBLE THREAT
Black to play and win

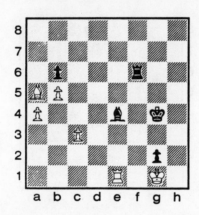

Black has visions of capturing White's bishop, but surely not at the expense of his own. Black could retreat his bishop to safety, but that grants White the time to do likewise with his.

The solution was **1. . . . Kf3!** [*DOUBLE THREAT*], which coaxed White's resignation (**0-1**), in view of the monster with two ugly heads: the capture of his bishop and the transfer of Black's rook to h6 and then to h1 for mate.

White can give up the exchange, 2. Rxe4, but after 2. . . . Kxe4 3. Bb4 Kf3, Black retains his mating net. If White retreats his bishop immediately, 2. Bb4, and then after 2. . . . Rh6 tries 3. Rxe4, 3. . . . Rh1 is still mate.

50

A. BELYAVSKY VS. G. KASPAROV
BARCELONA, SPAIN, 1989
WORLD CUP, ROUND 11

W: Kf4 Rc8 Bb5 Ps a4 e5   (5)
B: Ke7 Rh3 Bd4 Ps a5 e6 f7 g6   (7)

FORK
Black to play and win

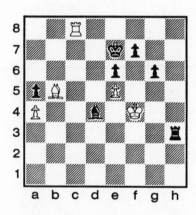

At first glance, Black seems to have a slight problem with his position: he is threatened with rook-mate at e8. Actually, with two pawns to the good, Black needs merely to survive the mate threat and the attendant menacing of his king. He did so by **1. . . . Rh4 +**.

White replied **2. Kg3,** with a two-pronged counterthreat: mate at e8 and capture of the rook at h4. White shunned 2. Kf3, for 2. . . . Bxe5 would have given Black escape squares at d6 and f6 while leaving him three pawns ahead.

Black's elegant answer was **2. . . . Rh8!,** and White

resigned (**1-0**), realizing that 3. Rxh8 would be squashed by 3. . . . Bxe5+ [*FORK*], giving check! Black then regains the rook and has an easily won endgame. White's futile 3. Rc7+ doesn't save him, for 3. . . . Kf8 4. Kf4 gains Black a third pawn by 4. . . . Rh5.

51

V. Salov vs. N. Short

BARCELONA, SPAIN, 1989
WORLD CUP, ROUND 2

W: Kf6 Qe8 (2)
B: Kh7 Ra7 (2)

FORK
White to play and win

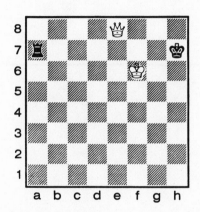

A classic. White to play has a forced win; the key is
to set up a fork by working the queen into a checking
position at b8 or g1 where it also attacks the rook. Play
proceeded **1. Qh5+ Kg8 2. Qg4+**, planning to zigzag
the queen into range by shifting it with checks from g4
to h3, to g3, to h2, and to b8).

There followed **2. ... Kh7** (if 2. ... Kf8, then
3. Qc8 mate) **3. Qh3+ Kg8 4. Qg3+**. But not 4. Qg2+,
when 4. ... Kf8 can't be answered with a safe check
along the eighth rank, for a8 is guarded by the rook.

Play continued: **4. ... Kh7** (or 4. ... Kh8 5. Qh2+
Rh7 6. Qb8 mate) **5. Qh2+ Kg8 6. Qb8+** [FORK] **6. ...
Kh7 7. Qxa7+ Kh8.**

Black doesn't fare better on 7. . . . Kh6 8. Qg7 + Kh5 9. Qg5 mate, delaying the inevitable for one move. The game halted after **8. Qg7 mate (1-0).**

White actually missed a faster victory from the diagram position, beginning with the centralizing check, 1. Qe4 + (book ending). After 1. . . . Kg8 2. Qd5 + Kh8 3. Qh1 + Kg8 (3. . . . Rh7 is mated by 4. Qa8 + +), 4. Qg1 + forks king and rook.

52

W: Kg1 Qc1 Ra5 Nd4 Nf2 Ps c3 d3 e5 g2 h2   (10)
B: Kg8 Qe7 Rc8 Rf8 Bb5 Ps a6 e6 g7 h7   (9)

FORK
Black to play and win

Black is slightly ahead in material: a rook and a bishop for two knights and a pawn. But White is threatening to gain a second pawn by capturing the bishop with his knight, and after Black recaptures the knight with the a-pawn, White's rook can take the new Black b-pawn.

Realizing the race is to the speedy, Black broke through by **1. . . . Rxf2!,** and White resigned (**0-1**).

If play continued 2. Kxf2 Qh4+ [*FORK*] 3. Kg1 (if 3. Ke3, Black skewers White's queen, 3. . . . Qg5+), Black can play 3. . . . Qxd4+ because White's c-pawn is pinned.

Suppose White eschews immediate capture on f2 and interpolates 2. Nxb5. After 2. . . . Rcf8 3. Nd4 Qg5! (double threat), Black threatens mate at g2 and c1. And if 4. Qxg5, Black mates by 4. . . . Rf1++.

53

J. Van der Weil vs. I. Sokolov
HANINGE, SWEDEN, 1989

W: Kh2 Qe6 Ps a2 b4 c3 f3 g2 h3   (8)
B: Kf8 Qb1 Nf2 Pb5   (4)

FORK
White to play and win

White to move can count on a draw. His queen can check the enemy king repeatedly, leading either to a threefold repetition of the same position or to what's commonly called "perpetual check." But why settle for a draw when a win is in sight?

The key is to capitalize on the "hanging" condition of Black's knight at f2, which White did, starting with **1. Qc8 +**. Black's king must move to his second rank, **1. . . . Kf7** (or 1. . . . Kg7 or 1. . . . Ke7). There followed **2. Qb7 +**, and Black resigned **(1-0)**.

White now maneuvers his queen onto a diagonal line with the knight, simultaneously giving check

[*FORK*]. After the king gets out of check, White captures the knight for nothing.

For example, if 2. . . . Kg6 (or 2. . . . Kf6 or 2. . . . Ke6), then 3. Qb6+ forks the king and knight. Or if 2. . . . Kg8 (or 2. . . . Kf8 or 2. . . . Ke8), then 3. Qa8+ followed by 4. Qa7+ accomplishes the same double attack.

54

V. Kotronias vs. A. Goldin
MOSCOW, USSR, 1989
GMA TOURNAMENT

W: Kg3 Qd7 Bc1 Ps b3 e4 g4 h3   (7)
B: Kg7 Re6 Bh1 Nc6 Ps a6 b5 f7 g6 h7   (9)

DOUBLE THREAT
White to play and win

Situation: White has a queen for a rook and a knight—advantage for White. But Black seems to have patched the holes in his position, with the f-pawn protecting the rook which in turn guards the knight. Black's bishop, meanwhile, scopes out White's e-pawn.

The solution is to undermine Black's linchpin, the f7-pawn. White achieved this by **1. Bh6 + !,** and Black resigned (**0-1**).

If Black accepts the bishop sacrifice, 1. . . . Kxh6, White pulls the rug out by 2 Qxf7 [*DOUBLE THREAT*], issuing powerful simultaneous attacks: to capture the rook on e6 and to mate by 3. Qf8 + Kg5 4. h4 + + (or 4. Qf4 + +).

If Black moves to defend his rook and the mate threat by 2. . . . Re7, then 3. Qf8+ Rg7 4. g5+ deflects the king from the rook's defense.

Black, of course, can turn down the bishop offering, but 1. . . . Kg8 2. Qc8+ leads to a back-rank mate in two moves.

55

V. IVANCHUK VS. E. TORRE
BIEL, SWITZERLAND, 1989

W: Kg1 Rd1 Ne4 Ng5 Ps c2 e7 f4 g2 h3   (9)
B: Kg7 Re8 Na3 Nb6 Ps f7 g6 h7   (7)

FORK
White to play and win

White's ace in the hole is the passed pawn at e7. But it's under fire from Black's rook and faces capture. Can it be saved?

You bet, by **1. f5!**, when 1. . . . Rxe7 drops a rook to the pawn fork, 2. f6 +. Black prevented this advance by moving his own f-pawn, **1. . . . f6.** He decided against 1. . . . gxf5 2. Nd6 Rxe7 3. Nxf5 + [*FORK*], attacking king and rook.

Black resigned after **2. Ne6 + (1-0)**, for his king doesn't have a safe square. If 2. . . . Kg8, then 3. Nxf6 + (fork) wins. Or 2. . . . Kh8, when 3. Nxf6 Rxe7 4. Rd8 + Re8 5. Rxe8 is mate. And if 2. . . . Kf7, then 3. Nd6 + (fork) also wins, as does 2. . . . Kh6 3. Nxf6 Rxe7 4. Ng8 + (fork).

56

L. Ljubojevic vs. J. Speelman

BARCELONA, SPAIN, 1989
WORLD CUP, ROUND 2

W: Kh2 Qe2 Bd3 Ps b2 h6   (5)
B: Kh7 Qd5 Ps a7 b6 f5   (5)

FORK
White to play and win

What force is here isn't much, but not much is required, and a unison of queen and bishop can be a potent team. Their capabilities were displayed after **1. Qe7 +**. One look at this incursion cowed Black into resignation (**1-0**).

What are his choices? His king can take the pawn or flee (but not to g8, because of mate, 2. Qg7 + +).

If 1. . . . Kxh6, then 2. Qf6 + Kh7 (or 2. . . . Kh5, leading to 3. Be2 + Qf3 4. Bxf3 + +, a criss-cross mate) 3. Bxf5 + Kg8 4. Be6 + [*FORK*] gains the queen for a bishop.

Maybe Black can try headlong flight, 1. . . . Kg6. That's a blind alley after 2. Qg7 + Kh5 3. Be2 + Qf3 4. Bxf3 + Kh4 5. Qg3 mate (or 5. Qf6 mate or 5. Qe7 mate).

57

E. Prie vs. L. Psakhis
PARIS, FRANCE, 1989

W: Ka1 Qg1 Rb1 Rg5 Nf5 Ps a2 b2 h6   (8)
B: Kh7 Qc2 Rc7 Rc8 Bb7 Bf8 Ps a6 b4   (8)

FORK
Black to play and win

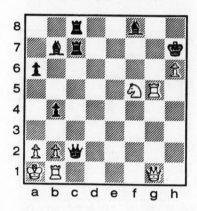

Weighing everything, the scales tip toward Black. He has two bishops against a knight and pawn, and his major pieces are tripled on the c-file, while White's are only doubled on the g-file. Even so, White has a semblance of g-file counterplay, so footsying around would be erroneous strategy. Black must act posthaste.

Indeed he did, playing **1. . . . Be4!** [*FORK*], blasting White into resignation (**0-1**).

White doesn't have a good defense. If 2. Rf1, getting the rook out on bail and adding protection to the knight, Black wins with 2. . . . Qc1+ 3. Rxc1 Rxc1+

4. Qxc1 Rxc1 + +. White's first rank is simply too vulnerable.

And if 2. Rg7 +, then 2. . . . Bxg7 3. hxg7 Qxb1 + (not 3. . . . Rxg7?? because of 4. Qxg7 mate) 4. Qxb1 Rc1 5. a3 b3, when mate follows shortly.

58

J. Ehlvest vs. J. Fedorowicz
NEW YORK, USA, 1989

W: Kg2 Qd8 Rb1 Bf3 Ps a3 d5 e2 f5 g4   (9)
B: Kg8 Qa4 Bf6 Ba6 Nf8 Ps c3 d6 e7 f7 g5   (10)

FORK
Black to play and win

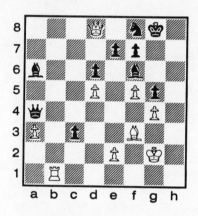

Black is materially ahead with a bishop and a knight for a rook, and his c-pawn is quite imposing. Things got even worse for White after **1. . . . Bxe2!**—so bad that he resigned **(0-1)**.

If White continues with the natural 2. Bxe2, then the double attack 2. . . . Qe4+ [*FORK*] gains the rook.

Surcease of sorrow still eludes White even after 2. Rb8, for 2. . . . Bxf3+ 3. Kxf3 Qf4+ gives Black the upper hand. He simply takes the g-pawn with check, maneuvers his queen to the e-file with check, and then retreats the bishop to g7, defending the knight. Black takes command.

59

A. Belyavsky vs. A. Karpov
Linares, Spain, 1989

W: Kh2 Qe7 Ng3 Ps e3 f3 g2 h4   (7)
B: Kg6 Qd5 Nb7 Ps c4 e6 f7 f5 h5   (8)

FORK
Black to play and win

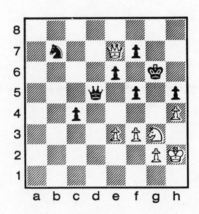

Black's c-pawn might become dangerous, but first he must deal with White's menacing queen check at g5. This was accomplished by **1. . . . Qd8!** (simplification), offering an exchange of queens, for such a reduction in force would augment the precious c-pawn's strength.

White refused the trade and took Black's knight, **2. Qxb7.** But Black regained the piece with the attack, **2. . . . Qxh4+** [*FORK*]. After **3. Kg1 Qxg3,** White saw nothing better than **4. Qb4.** Black mustered behind his c-pawn, supporting its advance by **4. . . . Qc7.**

White dogged on with **5. Qf8 c3 6. f4,** hoping for 7. Qg8+ Kf6 8. Qg5 mate. But after **6. . . . Kf6,** seeing no viable way to salvage a draw, White resigned **(0-1).**

5

PINS, PIN OVERLOADS, UNPINS, AND PILING ON

Players (White–Black)	Location
60. Polugaevsky–Kudrin	New York, USA
61. Christiansen–Nunn	West Germany
62. Gulko–Seirawan	Long Beach, USA
63. Westerinen–Zaitzev	Moscow, USSR
64. Yusupov–Short	Barcelona, Spain
65. Hansen–Sax	Lugano, Switzerland
66. Cebalo–Gurevich	Bern, Switzerland
67. Lerner–Vogt	Berlin, East Germany
68. Belyavsky–Ivanchuk	Linares, Spain

60

L. POLUGAEVSKY VS. S. KUDRIN
NEW YORK, USA, 1989
NEW YORK OPEN

W: Kg1 Qh7 Rh1 Bd4 Ps a2 d5 e4 f2 g2   (9)
B: Kf7 Qa6 Rf8 Bc4 Bg7 Ps a7 b7 f6 g6   (9)

PIN
White to play and win

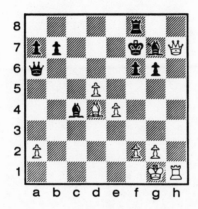

    White's chances look dim. He is behind in material: a pawn for Black's light-square bishop. Besides, Black has a trap in store. He could snare White's queen by Rh8, when the queen has no safe exit. But, as so often in life itself, success hinges on whose turn it is.

    White reaps the full benefit of having the move by **1. Rh6!** [*PIN*], and Black resigned (**1-0**). But why?

    Because what Black saw was 2. Rxg6 Rg8 (defending the g7-bishop) 3. Rxf6+, forking his king and queen. Here, the pinned g7-bishop is unable to lend a supportive hand to f6.

If, looking ahead, Black tries to deter this attack by
1. . . . Rg8, then 2. Qxg6+ Ke7 (on 2. . . . Kf8, he is
upset by 3. Bc5+) 3. Rh7 leaves White with a winning
position.

61

L. CHRISTIANSEN VS. J. NUNN
WEST GERMANY, 1989
WEST GERMAN TEAM CUP

W: Kg1 Rc1 Re1 Bf4 Nd5 Ne5 Ps d4 f2 g2 h2   (10)
B: Kd8 Ra8 Re8 Bb3 Be7 Nd6 Ps a6 b7 c7 f7 g7 h7   (12)

PIN OVERLOAD
White to play and win

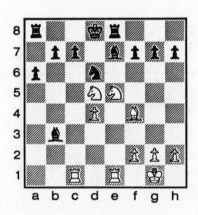

White is down two pawns, though his knight can take the c-pawn, forking Black's rooks and winning the exchange. Why play the second-best move when the first-best is best?

Black resigned (**1-0**) after **1. Nxf7 +!** [*PIN OVERLOAD*]. Question: To take or not to take the knight? If **1. . . . Nxf7**, White finishes with **2. Bxc7 + Kd7** (or **2. . . . Kc8 3. Nb6 mate**) **3. Nb6 mate.**

If Black declines the proffered f7-knight and responds **1. . . . Kd7**, then **2. Rxc7** is mate.

And on **1. . . . Kc8**, fleeing toward the queenside, White gains gobs of material with **2. Nxd6 +**, when both the c-pawn and e7-bishop are pinned.

62

B. Gulko vs. Y. Seirawan
LONG BEACH, CA, USA, 1989
U.S. CHAMPIONSHIP, ROUND 3

W: Kg1 Qc7 Rd1 Bc5 Bh3 Ps b6 e4 f2 g3 h2   (10)
B: Kg8 Qa6 Rb8 Rd8 Bd3 Ps a5 e5 f6 g7 h7   (10)

PIN
White to play and win

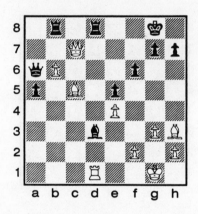

White is down the exchange (a bishop for a rook), though he has a potential nuisance in his far-advanced passed b-pawn. Moreover, his two bishops provide nasty attacking chances, if Black gives them the chance. Black's bishop is pinned on the d-file. This is important, for moving it off exposes the d8-rook to humiliating capture.

The jackal is the withdrawal, **1. Bf1** [*PIN*], menacing an exchange on d3, drawing the d8-rook away from protection of the other rook. Black safeguarded the rook—with an apparent gain of time—*1. . . . Rbc8.* But White blandly ignored this attack to his queen and carried out his own threat, **2. Bxd3!**. If Black now captures White's queen, **2. . . . Rxc7**, White forges the win with **3. bxc7!**, when **3. . . . Rxd3 4. Rxd3** insures the c-pawn's promotion.

Black took White's bishop instead, **2. . . . Rxd3,** but after **3. Rxd3 Rxc7 4. Rd8+**, Black resigned (**1-0**).

63

H. WESTERINEN VS. I. ZAITZEV
MOSCOW, USSR, 1989
REGIONAL B TOURNAMENT

W: Kh1 Rg1 Bb3 Ps a2 b2 c3 d4 d6 h2   (9)
B: Kf7 Re6 Rg8 Ng4 Ps a6 b5 c7 h7   (8)

PILING ON
White to play and win

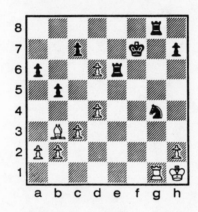

Even with a winning position it's easy to go wrong. Here, if White were tempted into playing 1. Re1?, piling on the pinned e6-rook, he would encounter the unpleasant 1. . . . Nf2! mate.

White's first move eliminates that sting, while setting up a clear gain of material based on the pin. White shifted **1. Rf1 + !.** Now if 1. . . . Ke8, the e6-rook is left unprotected to the attack of the b3-bishop.

Black replied to the check by **1. . . . Nf6,** blocking the check and taking the knight out of position for counterplay, allowing **2. Re1** [*PILING ON*].

Black resigned (**1-0**), for 2. . . . Re8 3. Rxe6 Rxe6 4. dxc7 is decisive—a new queen will soon emerge at c8.

64

A. Yusupov vs. N. Short
BARCELONA, SPAIN, 1989
WORLD CUP, ROUND 10

W: Kg1 Qa4 Re1 Rd5 Bb3 Nf3 Ps a3 b2 e5 f2 g2 h3 (12)
B: Kg7 Qb6 Rd7 Re8 Be7 Be6 Ps a7 c5 f7 g6 h6   (11)

UNPIN
Black to play and win

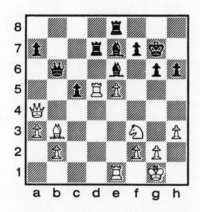

Pawns mean something. Count them. Black has one less than White. Besides, his rooks are skewered by White's queen along the a4-e8 diagonal. If the d7-rook moves, the e8-rook is exposed to attack.

But White has problems, too. The rook at d5 is subject to capture, as is the b3-bishop, now guarded by the queen.

If Black captures the d5-rook, 1. . . . Bxd5, then White stands well after 2. Qxd7 Rd8 (2. . . . Bc6 3. Qd3 saves the queen and upholds b3) 3. Qxe7 Bxb3 4. e6 (pin) 4. . . . Bxe6 5. Rxe6 (overload), when Black's queen can't simultaneously defend d8 and capture on e6. The line 1. . . . Rxd5 2. Bxd5 is undesirable also, for White stays a pawn ahead.

Black pieced the winning line together by 1. . . . **Red8!** [*UNPIN*], after which the Black rooks protected each other. A skewer followed **2. Rxd7 Bxd7 3. Oc4 Be6,** and white resigned **(0-1)**, for his b3-bishop is dead meat.

65

L. HANSEN vs. G. SAX
LUGANO, SWITZERLAND, 1989

W: Kg1 Qb1 Re1 Bh3 Ps a2 b3 f2 g3 h2   (9)
B: Kg8 Qa3 Re8 Be2 Ps a7 b6 d4 f7 g7 h7   (10)

PIN
White to play and win

Black's bishop is pinned on the e-file, rook to rook. Two reasonable defenses arise on the waters: advancing the d-pawn to d3 and retreating the e2-bishop to b5, where it defends the e8-rook.

Unfortunately, neither one works after **1. Bf1!** [*PIN*]. The advance 1. . . . d3 fails to 2. Qxd Bxd3 3. Rxe8+ Qf8 4. Rxf8+ Kxf8 5. Bxd3; and the retreat 1. . . . Bb5 succumbs to 2. Bxb5.

So Black hauled out **1. . . . Qa6,** resigning after **2. Rxe2 (1–0).** A natural continuation is 2. . . . Rxe2 3. Qd1 d3 4. Bxe2, winning a rook (pin), for 4. . . . dxe2 permits 5. Qd8 mate.

66

M. CEBALO VS. M. GUREVICH
BERN, SWITZERLAND, 1989

W: Kg1 Qb5 Rd2 Rd1 Be3 Ps a4 e4 f2 g2 h2   (10)
B: Kg8 Qc4 Rc8 Rd8 Bf8 Ps a7 b6 d4 f6 g7 h7   (11)

UNPIN
Black to play and win

Black's d-pawn is attacked three times (two rooks and a bishop) and guarded only twice (queen and rook). Worse: it's pinned on the d-file to the d8-rook. How does Black cope? This problem is potentially debilitating.

First Black eliminates a major attacker/defender, the White queen, **1. . . . Qxb5** (removing the guard) **2. axb5.** The queens gone, White's back rank is suddenly more vulnerable, constraining him to resign **(0-1)** after the surprising **2. . . . dxe3!** [*UNPIN*].

If White tries to win a rook (3. Rxd8 Rxd8 4. Rxd8), Black makes a new queen (4. . . . e2), for White's remaining rook cannot stumble back to stop the pawn.

And if White doesn't take the second rook and defends with 4. Re1 instead, Black consummates his play with 4. . . . e2, when 5. f3 Bc5+ 6. Kh1 Rd1 (promotion) is decisive.

67

K. Lerner vs. L. Vogt
BERLIN, EAST GERMANY, 1989

W: Kg2 Qf3 Re2 Re1 Bd5 Bh6 Ps a2 b2 c4 f2 g4 h3 (12)
B: Kg8 Qd7 Rb8 Re8 Be6 Be5 Ps a7 b7 c5 d6 g6 h7 (12)

PIN
White to play and win

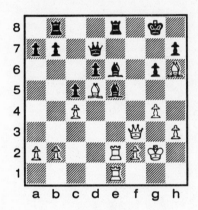

What an e-file! Doubled White rooks, Black bishops in potential pins. If only White could make the e5-bishop vamoose.

The win was achieved by **1. Qe4!**, threatening 2. f4, dislodging the e5-bishop [*PIN*].

Now Black might have tried 1. . . . Qf7, leading to 2. f4 Bxd5 3. cxd5 Bg7 4. Qxe8+ Rxe8 5. Rxe8+ Qxe8 6. Rxe8+ Kf7 7. Bxg7 (simplification), with a winning game.

Black actually played **1. . . . Bxd5,** and after **2. Qxd5+,** resigned **(1-0)**. If 2. . . . Qf7, then 3. f4 capitalizes on the pinned f7-queen and on the e-file pin. Or if 2. . . . Kh8 instead, then 3. Rxe5 does the trick, since the d6-pawn is pinned.

Three pins were prominent in the above lines: on the e-file, on the f7-queen, and on the d6-pawn.

68

A. BELYAVSKY VS. V. IVANCHUK
LINARES, SPAIN, 1989

W: Kd1 Qe4 Rb5 Rd4 Be3 Nf3 Ps a2 c4 h2   (9)
B: Ke8 Qg2 Ra8 Rg8 Bc8 Be7 Ps a7 b7 c7 f7   (10)

PIN
Black to play and win

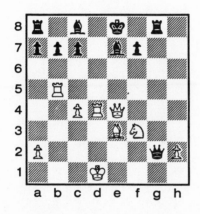

Neither side is castled, the center is wide open, and all the major pieces (except the a8-rook) are actively placed. There's trouble in store for the player who goes second, in this case White. White got a migraine after **1. . . . Bg4** [*PIN*].

White could hold the fort only with **2. Rf5,** offering a rook for a bishop to break the pernicious pin on the d1-h5 diagonal. The interpolation **2. . . . Qf1+,** however, forced the concession **3. Kc2,** shoving the king onto the same b1-h7 diagonal as the queen.

What else is there? On 3. Kd2 Bxf5 4. Qxf5 Rg2+ 5. Kc3 Qa1+, Black mates in three more moves: either by 6. Kb3 Qxa2+ 7. Kc3 Qb2+ 8. Kd3 Qc2++; or by

6. Kd3 Qb1+ 7. Kc3 Qb2+ 8. Kd3 Qc2++. In either variation, White goes down with the same mate.

After the actual 3. Kc2, Black inched closer, **3. . . . Qe2+**, and White resigned (**0-1**). He can lose in several ways: 4. Rd2 Bxf5 (deflection) 5. Qxf5 Qxe3; or 4. Bd2 Qxe4 (removing the guard) 5. Rxe4 Bxf5 (pin).

6

SKEWERS AND DISCOVERIES

Players (White–Black)	Location
69. Christiansen–Peters	Los Angeles, CA, USA
70. Nikolic-Plchut	Correspondence
71. Kasparov–Short	Barcelona, Spain
72. Short–Vaganyan	Barcelona, Spain
73. Kouatly–Kasparov	Paris, France
74. Gulko–Belyavsky	Linares, Spain

69

L. CHRISTIANSEN VS. J. PETERS

LOS ANGELES, CA, USA, 1989
LINA GRUMETTE MEMORIAL DAY CLASSIC

W: Kg4 Rh3 Nb6 Ps a2 b4 c5 e6 f5 (8)
B: Ke8 Rc7 Nd5 Ps a6 b5 c6 f6 g5 (8)

SKEWER
White to play and win

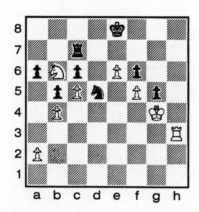

The highway of success seems to be White's control of the open h-file. Traveling its true path, he can force a trade of rooks and knights. But the resulting endgame lacks clarity, both sides retaining passed pawns.

The winning line was established by using the h-file only on the first move, **1. Rh8+ Ke7,** and following the rook tickler, **2. Na8!,** Black resigned **(1-0)**, facing a loss of at least a rook for a knight, leading to an early defeat.

Black can't save his rook by either 2. . . . Rb7 or 2. . . . Ra7 because White picks it off along Route 66, **3. Rh7+** [*SKEWER*]. After Black's king moves out of check, his rook is captured for nothing. QED.

70

B. NIKOLIC VS. PLCHUT
CORRESPONDENCE GAME, 1989

W: Ke1 Qb3 Rb1 Rg1 Bc1 Bf1 Ne2 Ps a3 d3 f6 f5 g4 h2 (13)

B: Kc8 Qc7 Rd8 Re8 Bd7 Ne5 Nh4 Ps a7 b6 (9)

DISCOVERY
Black to play and win

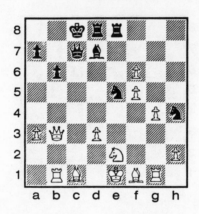

Even loaded with four extra pawns, White is far behind in development and his king is exposed to attack along the central files. Black clinched the issue with **1. . . . Ba4.** After assaying the consequences of accepting Black's proffered bishop, White opted to throw in the towel *(0-1).*

If the bishop sacrifice is accepted, 2. Qxa4, then 2. . . . Nxd3+ 3. Kd1 (or 3. Kd2) 3. . . . Nc5+ [*DISCOVERY*] wins White's queen by uncovering an attack on his king by the d8-rook.

If the bishop sacrifice is declined, say by 2. Qc3, then 2. . . . Qxc3+ 3. Nxc3 Nxd3+ (discovery) 4. Kd2 Nf3 is mate.

71

G. Kasparov vs. N. Short

BARCELONA, SPAIN, 1989
WORLD CUP, ROUND 8

W: Kf3 Rd1 Re6 Ne4 Ps a4 f6 f4   (7)
B: Kf8 Re2 Rh2 Ne8 Ps a5 c5 g6   (7)

DISCOVERY
White to play and win

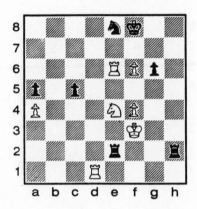

Black has leashed-up rooks doubled on his seventh rank, their power so far held in abeyance. Contrariwise, White's rooks dominate the files, and the f6-pawn is rather menacing.

Things erupted after **1. f7!**, when 1. ... Kxf7 **2. Ng5+** [*DISCOVERY*] gains the e2-rook. A similar result follows 1. ... Nc7 2. Rd8+ Kxf7 3. Ng5+ (discovery).

So Black tried **1. ... Rhf2+**, but resigned **(1-0)** after **2. Nxf2 Rxe6 3. fxe8/Q+ Kxe8 4. Rc1.** He's a knight down with no compensation.

72

N. SHORT VS. R. VAGANYAN

BARCELONA, SPAIN
WORLD CUP, ROUND 3, 1989

W: Kg1 Qf8 Rc7 Bg3 Ps a4 f2 g2 h3   (8)
B: Kg6 Qd4 Rg7 Be4 Ps a6 b7 g5   (7)

SKEWER
White to play and win

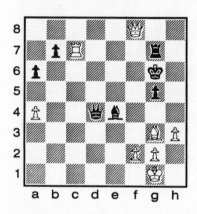

In an endgame, bishops of opposite colors often lead to a draw, even if one side is ahead by a couple of pawns. This can happen if the inferior side manages to set up a blockade impenetrable by the opposing bishop. But in the middlegame, in attack formations, opposite-color bishops may be an advantage for the side with the initiative, for the defending bishop could be helpless to guard the attacking bishop's targets.

Here, Black never reached an endgame, for White won material with **1. Rxg7+ Qxg7 2. Qe8+ Kf5 3. Qc8+ Kf6?.**

Black drops the bishop anyway after 3. . . . Kg6 **4. Qe6+** (fork). After **4. Be5+!** [*SKEWER*], Black resigned **(1-0)**, for 4. . . . Kxe5 is squelched by another skewer, 5. Qc3+.

B. KOUATLY VS. G. KASPAROV
PARIS, FRANCE, JUNE 1989
SIMULTANEOUS CLOCK EXHIBITION

W: Kg2 Qd2 Rb1 Rg4 Be3 Be2 Nc3 Nf1 Ps a2 c4 d5 g5
(12)

B: Kg8 Qf7 Re8 Rf8 Be5 Bg6 Nd3 Ps b2 b7 c7 d6 e4 h7
(13)

DISCOVERY
Black to play and win

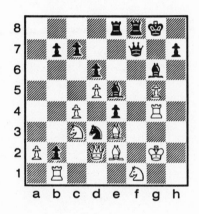

Black has sacrificed a piece for two pawns and the attack. His control of the f-file, his powerfully poised pieces, and his far-advanced pawn on b2 add up to a winning position.

Black played **1. . . . Nf4 +**, when the knight must be captured for fear of 2. . . . Bxc3 3. Qxc3 Nxe2. After **2. Bxf4,** Black interpolates **2. . . . e3!** [*DISCOVERY*], to open the e-file and clear the g6-bishop's diagonal, attacking the rook on b1.

The game continued **3. Bxe3 Bxc3** (removing the guard of the b1-rook) **4. Qxc3 Bxb1** (threatening 5. . . .

Be4+ and 6. . . . b1/Q) **5. Rf4** (hoping to guard the f-file by gaining time with an attack on the queen) **5. . . . Rxe3!** (removing the guard), and White resigned **(0-1)**. If 6. Nxe3 or 6. Qxe3, then 6. . . . Qxf4 puts Black clearly ahead. If 6. Rxf7 instead, then 6. . . . Rxc3 is equally good, and Black should gain even more material shortly.

B. GULKO VS. A. BELYAVSKY
LINARES, SPAIN, 1989

W: Kf4 Qg2 Rd3 Be5 Ps a2 b3 d4 g4 h4   (9)
B: Ka7 Qc8 Ra1 Ba3 Ps a6 b7 d5 g6 h5   (9)

SKEWER
Black to play and win

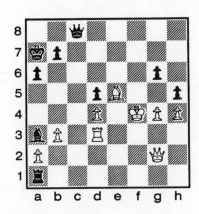

What a fight—queens and rooks on an open board! Quite treacherous for the king on f4. There are a number of ways to ax White's rex. Which is the surest? Probably it's the one beginning with **1. . . . Rf1 + !**, for White didn't bother to play on **(0-1)**. Then 2. Qxf1 loses the queen, 2. . . . Qf8 + [*SKEWER*].

White can continue only by moving his king. On 2. Kg3, Black's 2. . . . Qxg4 + 3. Kh2 Qxh4 + is devastating. If instead 2. Ke3, then Black gets a winning attack by 2. . . . Qc1 + 3. Qd2 Qb1 (threatening to pin the queen by Bc1) 4. Qa5 hxg4 5. Ke2 Rg1 6. Ke3 Qf1.

Finally, White might try to flee by 2. Kg5, but Black's 2. . . . Bc1 + 3. Kxg6 Qe8 + 4. Kh7 Qf7 + 5. Bg7 Rf6, planning to mate at h6 (pin), would force White's resignation.

7

OVERLOADS, REMOVING THE GUARDS, AND DEFLECTIONS

Players (White–Black)	Location
75. Cetverik–Krysanov	USSR
76. Piket–Sax	Wijk aan Zee, Netherlands
77. Salov–Vaganyan	Barcelona, Spain
78. Sillman–Christiansen	Los Angeles, CA, USA
79. Spraggett–Yusupov	Quebec City, Canada
80. Rohde–Brooks	Las Vegas, NV, USA
81. Belyavsky–Korchnoi	Barcelona, Spain
82. Anand–Spassky	Cannes, France
83. Gavrilov–Berdishevsky	USSR
84. Short–Illescas	Barcelona, Spain
85. Korchnoi–Nikolic	Barcelona, Spain
86. Simic–Krasenkov	Ptuj, Yugoslavia
87. Garcia–Westerinen	Alicante, Spain
88. Ehlvest–Hjartarson	Rotterdam, Netherlands

75

W: Kc1 Qe5 Rg6 Be6 Nc3 Ps a3 b2 e3 f2 h4   (10)
B: Kf8 Qe7 Rh8 Rh5 Na6 Ps a7 b6 c6   (8)

OVERLOAD
White to play and win

No pawns shielding the Black king is a telling sign. White could easily go astray and start checking. Perhaps a queen check at f4 and a rook check at f6, but neither are as effective as the simple **1. Qxh5!**, which coerced Black to give up **(0-1)**.

White has a brutal point: that Black can't take White's queen [*OVERLOAD*], 1. . . . Rxh5, because of the counter 2. Rg8 mate. Otherwise, Black has no desperados, and no hope.

J. Piket vs. G. Sax
WIJK AAN ZEE, NETHERLANDS, 1989

W: Kg1 Qf3 Ra1 Rb5 Bb2 Bc4 Ps a2 b3 e2 f2 g3 h2 (12)
B: Kg8 Qe7 Rc6 Rd8 Bc5 Na6 Ps a7 b7 f7 g6 h7 (11)

REMOVING THE GUARD
White to play and win

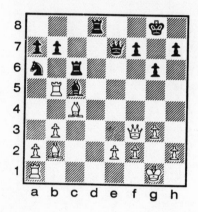

White's bishops rake the kingside, with the b2-bishop dominating the a1-a8 diagonal and the c4-bishop attacking and pinning the f7-pawn. White must not play the rash 1. Qc3?, which would be rebuffed by the blunt 1. . . . Bd4. To avert this block, White annihilated the blocker by capture, **1. Rxc5!** [*REMOVING THE GUARD*].

Black resigned **(1-0)**, for whether 1. . . . Rxc5 or 1. . . . Nxc5, White follows with 2. Qc3 (mating attack), issuing decisive threats on the long dark diagonal. Of course 1. . . . Qxc5 permits the definitive 2. Qxf7 mate.

V. SALOV VS. R. VAGANYAN

BARCELONA, SPAIN, 1989
WORLD CUP, ROUND 7

W: Kd1 Rd7 Nf7 Ps g3 h4   (5)
B: Kf6 Rb3 Ne4 Ps a4 f5 h5   (6)

OVERLOAD
Black to play and win

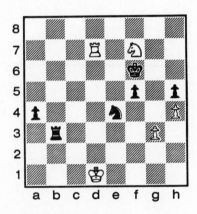

An even position materially, except for the passed
Black a-pawn, which actually makes it quite uneven.
Black drove home his advantage by **1. . . . a3**, threaten-
ing to produce a new queen pronto.

To frustrate its promotion to the head of the class,
White had to position his rook behind the passed
pawn—generally the best place for a rook, unless like
this one it has to keep a watchful eye on the insecure
f7-knight.

After **2. Ra7**, Black continued the big push, **2. . . .
a2**, realizing that 3. Rxa2 gets forked by 3. . . . Nc3+.
Moreover, if the rook moves off the seventh rank, the
knight flops. If White tries to rescue the knight, ending

this predicament, Black wins by checking on b1, following with promotion at a1.

White strove with **3. Kc2,** but that failed to the stifling **3. . . . Rb7!** [*OVERLOAD*]. At the very least, White had to drop the knight, so he resigned (**0-1**).

78

W: Kf3 Rb1 Bb8 Ps d5 g4 h4   (6)
B: Kd7 Ba6 Bd2 Ps c5 d6 e7 e3 h7   (8)

OVERLOAD
Black to play and win

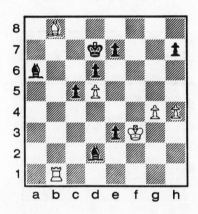

White has a rook for a bishop, though Black has two extra pawns. The one at e3 is a serious menace, especially convoyed by two bishops. White has another worry. He has to extricate his bishop, blocked in by Black pawns.

Black took advantage of his strengths by **1. . . . e2,** which forced **2. Kf2.** The ensuing **2. . . . Bd3 3. Ra1 Kc8 4. Ba7 Kb7** [*OVERLOAD*], compelled White to resign **(0-1).**

The e-pawn soon promotes. White will have to exchange a rook for a bishop and new queen, after which the a7-bishop is lost.

79

K. Spraggett vs. A. Yusupov
QUEBEC CITY, CANADA, 1989
CANDIDATES MATCH, GAME 2

W: Kg1 Qc2 Rc8 Bg2 Ne4 Ps a6 d4 g3   (8)
B: Kh7 Qf5 Rb4 Re7 Ps g7 h6   (6)

DEFLECTION
White to play and win

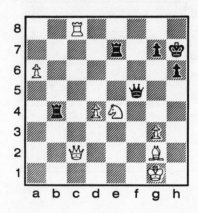

Let's review White's assets: a material advantage (a bishop, a knight, a pawn against a rook), a far-advanced passed pawn on a6, and the initiative. Of great significance is the b1-h7 diagonal. If Black's queen were not on it, White could discover mate.

White's can-opener **1. g4!** [*DEFLECTION*] compelled **1. . . . Qg6,** keeping the diagonal closed and avoiding 1. . . . Qxg4 2. Nf6 mate or 2. Ng5 mate.

The game concluded: **2. Nf6 + gxf6 3. Rh8 +** (deflection), and Black resigned (**1-0**). If 3. . . . Kg7 (3. . . . Kxh8 drops the queen, 4. Qxg6), then 4. Rg8 + (skewer) gains milady anyway.

M. ROHDE VS. M. BROOKS

LAS VEGAS, NV, 1989
NATIONAL OPEN

W: Kg1 Qg3 Ra1 Rb1 Bd5 Ps e4 g2 h3   (8)
B: Kh8 Qd6 Ra6 Rd8 Bh6 Ps c5 d4 e5 h7   (9)

DEFLECTION
White to play and win

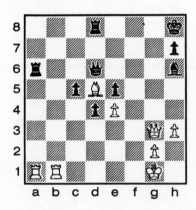

The players have bishops of opposite colors, which is an advantage for the attacker—White—because his light-square bishop cannot be neutralized by Black's dark-square one. Also, Black's pieces are not coordinating smoothly. White's, on the other hand, are cogs in a well-oiled machine, each doing a job.

White began with the reducing **1. Rxa6 Qxa6,** and followed with **2. Rb8!** [*DEFLECTION*], exploiting Black's lack of coordination. If 2. . . . Rxb8, then 3. Qxe5+ forks the king and rook, when 3. . . . Bg7 4. Qxb8+ forces mate. So Black's third move must ditch the queen, 3. . . . Qf6, to avert mate.

In the actual game, Black defended the e-pawn and the rook by **2. . . . Qd6,** but that failed to **3. Qg8 +!** (back rank). Black resigned (**1-0**), for 3. . . . Rxg8 allows 4. Rxg8 mate.

A. BELYAVSKY VS. V. KORCHNOI

BARCELONA, SPAIN, 1989
WORLD CUP, ROUND 11

W: Ka2 Rb1 Rd1 Be4 Ps a3 b4 b2 g2 h2   (9)
B: Kf8 Rc2 Rd8 Be5 Ps a4 f7 f4 g5 h6   (9)

OVERLOAD
Black to play and win

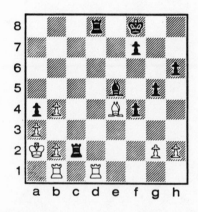

Here, both Black rooks are hanging, subject to immediate capture. Black could save himself by 1. . . . Rxd1 2. Bxc2 Rd2, but White would still have some fight.

Sometimes taking the offensive is the best defense. Black could exploit White's burdened b1-rook, which is guarding both b2 and d1 [*OVERLOAD*]. This he actually did by **1. . . . Rxb2 + !**, and White resigned **(0-1)**.

After 2. Rxb2 Rxd1, White's rook cannot move without serious consequences. If it moves along the second rank, then Black mates at a1. If instead 3. Rb1, then 3. . . . Rd2+ is crushing.

No better is 3. Bf3 Rc1 4. Rd2 Ra1 mate. And if White answers 1. . . . Rxb2+ by 2. Ka1, then Black scores with a discovery, 2. . . . Rf2+.

82

V. Anand vs. B. Spassky

CANNES, FRANCE
TOURNAMENT OF GENERATIONS, 1989

W: Kg1 Nc5 Nc3 Ps a5 b3 g2   (6)
B: Kf4 Bf7 Nb4 Ps g6 h5   (5)

DEFLECTION
White to play and win

White's passed a-pawn is menacing, needing only three moves to queen. If White advances precipitately, **1. a6?**, Black surrenders his knight for the a-pawn and afterward his bishop captures the b-pawn. Thereupon a draw seems likely.

The winning move was **1. Nd3 +!** [*DEFLECTION*]. After the compulsory **1. . . . Nxd3,** Black's knight was displaced, unable to overtake White's a-pawn, **2. a6** (promotion).

Black tried to reposition his bishop to c6, controlling the queening square, **2. . . . Be8,** but that plan was bushwhacked by **3. Nd5 +.** Black gave up **(1-0),** for **3. . . . Ke5** fails to 4. Ne7 (shut off), when c6 is guarded by the knight. The undeterrable a-pawn thunders on.

83

A. Gavrilov vs. Berdishevsky
USSR, 1989

W: Kh1 Qb3 Rb1 Rd1 Bf4 Bf3 Nb5 Ps c4 g4 g3 h2   (11)
B: Kg8 Qh3 Ra8 Rg6 Bc5 Be4 Ps b6 b4 d7 f7 g7 h7   (12)

OVERLOAD
Black to play and win

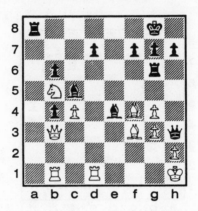

Black is fully armed: aligned bishops bearing on White's kingside, an entrenched queen at h3, and two mobile rooks. White's extra knight is of little consequence. The real key is his exposed king, with insufficient pawn-cover.

Black's panzer struck with **1. ... Ra2!**, menacing mate at h2. His rook is immune to capture because White's queen is too burdened and cannot leave the f3-bishop hanging [*OVERLOAD*].

So White thwarted the h2-mate threat by blocking the second rank, **2. Rd2.** White would err with the block 2. Bd2, for Black could then play 2. ... Rh6 with impunity since the d2-bishop is shielding h2.

After 2. . . . **Rxd2 3. Bxd2,** Black countered 3. . . . **Rf6!,** threatening the f3-bishop and, by x-ray, a rook-check on f1. White tried to block out the rook by 4. **Bf4,** but Black took it anyway, 4. . . . **Rxf4!** (pin). Since 5. gxf4 subjects the f3-bishop to Black's queen, White resigned **(0-1).**

N. SHORT VS. M. ILLESCAS

BARCELONA, SPAIN, 1989
WORLD CUP, ROUND 7

W: Kd4 Rf4 Nd5 Ps a4 b6 e4 g4   (7)
B: Kd7 Rg5 Rg2 Ps a5 d6   (5)

DEFLECTION
White to play and win

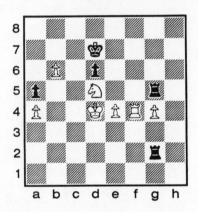

Black is up the exchange (a rook for a knight), but he's not home free, for White has two additional pawns. The one on b6 is a dangerous passed pawn, demanding surveillance by Black.

White obviously intended to queen a pawn after **1 b7.** To stop it Black had to respond **1. . . . Rb2,** positioning his rook behind the passed pawn. Guarding b8 by moving the rook back to g8 loses to 2. Nf6 + (fork).

The win was fashioned by **2. Rf7 +,** and Black withdrew his king, **2. . . . Ke8.** But not to 2. . . . Kc6 3. Rc7 mate. A similar setup results from 2. . . . Ke6 3. Re7

mate. Neither does 2. . . . Kd8 save the day, for 3. Rf8 +
seizes control of b8, forcing Black to sacrifice his b2-
rook once the pawn reaches the last rank.
The final moves were **3. Re7 +! Kd8 4. Kc3! Rb1
5. Kc2** and, with his rook forced off the b-file [*DEFLEC-
TION*], Black resigned (**1-0**).

85

V. KORCHNOI VS. P. NIKOLIC
BARCELONA, SPAIN, 1989
WORLD CUP, ROUND 1

W: Kg1 Qf5 Rc1 Rf1 Bd4 Be2 Ps a2 b3 c4 f6 g2 h2 (12)
B: Kh8 Qf7 Ra8 Rc8 Ba6 Bh6 Ne8 Ps a5 b4 d5 g5 h7
(12)

DEFLECTION
White to play and win

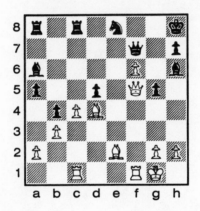

White should be in clover with a kingside assault, a dangerous passed pawn, and a bishop poised for discovering on Black's king. The sneaky weed is Black's queen sitting in front of the f-pawn as a blockade. Voila! Enter **1. Bh5!** [*DEFLECTION*].

Rather than lose at once, Black retreated his harried queen, **1. . . . Qf8.** Why didn't the queen take the bishop instead? Because 1. . . . Qxh5? 2, 17 + (discovery) 2. . . . Ng7 3. f8/Q + Rxf8 4. Qxf8 + Rxf8 5. Rxf8 is definitively mate.

Neither is counterattack, 1. . . . Nd6, a satisfactory

response, for 2. Bxf7 Nxf5 3. Rxf5 dxc4 4. Bd5 Rab8 5. Rxg5 also leads to a kill.

Back to the actual game, where White answered Qf8 by **2. Bxe8,** which moved Black to resign **(1-0)**. No reply can cope with the upcoming discovery, f6-f7 + .

86

R. SIMIC VS. M. KRASENKOV
PTUJ, YUGOSLAVIA, 1989

W: Kg1 Qe6 Rf1 Rh4 Be4 Ps f2 g3 (7)
B: Kh8 Qd4 Rf8 Rg7 Nb4 Ps c7 c2 h7 (8)

OVERLOAD
Black to play and win

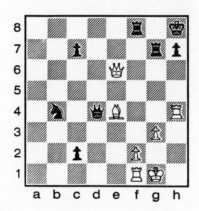

It could be a shootout, with each side's pieces ready with loaded guns. But Black has the first move, and a rather menacing passed c2-pawn. The latter decided the outcome after the shot, **1. . . . Rxf2!**, and rather than waste bullets, White resigned **(0-1)**.

Does White have a semblance of resistance? He might take the rook, 2. Rxf2 [*OVERLOAD*], but that abandons his first rank, resulting in 2. . . . Rxg3+ 3. Bg2 c1/Q+ 4. Kh2 Qxh4+ 5. Qh3 Qxh3+ (clearance) 6. Bxh3 Qg1 mate.

No relief is offered by 2. Qe8+, either, for the block, 2. . . . Rf8+ (discovery), wins White's queen. Moreover, the line 2. Rxh7+ Rxh7 3. Rxf2 c1/Q+ 4. Kg2 Qh1 is mate, also not too appetizing for White.

J. Fernandez Garcia vs. H. Westerinen
ALICANTE, SPAIN, 1989
ALICANTE OPEN

W: Kh4 Rc1 Rf2 Bf6 Ps a2 b2 c4 e5 f4 g4 h3   (11)
B: Ke6 Rb4 Ba5 Be4 Ps a4 c5 c7 d3 f7 f5 h7   (11)

OVERLOAD
Black to play and win

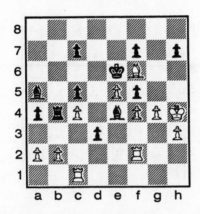

It matters little that White is up the exchange. Black has two potentially dangerous bishops and a threatening passed d-pawn. White's rooks, moreover, coordinating poorly, are out to lunch.

Black crowned his play with **1. . . . Rxc4!** [*OVERLOAD*], and White, seeing the handwriting on the wall, resigned (**0-1**).

If White captures the rook, 2. Rxc4, he hands over control of e1, allowing 2. . . . Be1! (pin) 3. Kg3 d2, and the pawn promotes.

White can refuse the rook capture, say 2. Rd1, but the advantage is Black's via 2. . . . Rc2 3. Kg3 c4 (opening the a7-g1 diagonal) 4. a3 (otherwise Black plays a4-a3, obtaining connected passed pawns) 4. . . . Bb6 5. Rh2 Bd4 6. Rb1 Be3.

88

J. Ehlvest vs. J. Hjartarson

ROTTERDAM, NETHERLANDS, 1989
WORLD CUP TOURNAMENT, ROUND 15

W: Kg2 Qg4 Rb7 Bb4 Bd5 Ps c4 e2 f2 g3 h2   (10)
B: Kh8 Qa1 Rc8 Rg8 Nc2 Ps a4 e5 g7 h7   (9)

OVERLOAD
White to play and win

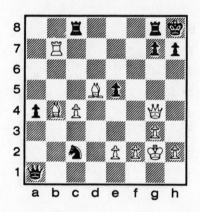

Black is up the exchange. White can regain a rook for a bishop by 1. Bxg8, which may win for White after he irons out a few kinks, such as the relentless advance a4-a3 and the pesky Nc2-e1+.

White eschewed intricacies, cutting the Gordian Knot with **1. Rxg7!.** Black resigned **(1-0)** in view of 1. . . . Rxg7 [*OVERLOAD*] 2. Qxc8+ and mate next move.

If Black tries to clear g8 instead, say 1. . . . Rgd8, then 2. Rxh7+ (mating net) 2. . . . Kxh7 3. Qh5+ Kg7 4. Qg5+ Kh7 (4. . . . Kh8 allows 5. Qh6 mate) 5. Be4+ Kh8 6. Qh6+ Kg8 7. Qh7 is mate.

8

SIMPLIFICATIONS, PROMOTIONS, SHUT OFFS, BOOK ENDINGS, AND TECHNIQUE

Players (White–Black)	Location
89. Van der Sterren–Gelfand	Amsterdam, Netherlands
90. Lobron–Greenfeld	Rogaska Slatina, Yugoslavia
91. Schlosser–Petursson	Munich, West Germany
92. Popovic–Bagirov	Moscow, USSR
93. Koch–Wilder	Cannes, France
94. Dreev–Geller	Moscow, USSR
95. Belov–Strikovic	Pula, Yugoslavia
96. Fedorowicz–Ivanov	Long Beach, CA, USA
97. Stohl–Reyes	Vrnjacka Banja, Yugoslavia
98. Korchnoi–Kasparov	Barcelona, Spain
99. Petursson–Sherzer	Philadelphia, PA, USA
100. Velimirovic–Damjanovic	Zenica, Yugoslavia

P. Van der Sterren vs. B. Gelfand
AMSTERDAM, NETHERLANDS, 1989
OHRA GM GROUP

W: Kh1 Qd8 Rd1 Ps d7 e4 g2 h3   (7)
B: Kh7 Qf4 Be5 Ph6   (4)

SIMPLIFICATION
White to play and win

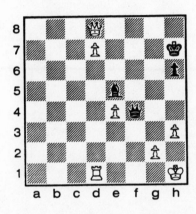

Ahead the exchange (a rook for a bishop), White is about to make a new queen—if he can ward off mate at h2, courtesy of Black's queued-up queen and bishop. But there's no apparent way to protect h2, and shifting the king to g1 doesn't elude Black's checks.

The winning procedure commences with a queen check, **1. Qe7+.** Black responded **1. . . . Kg6.** Rather than continue checking, White broke Black's attack, and his back, with **2. Qxe5!** [*SIMPLIFICATION*].

If you have a big material advantage and are under attack, it makes sense to give back some material, thwarting counterplay and reducing the position to a clear win.

Black resigned (**1-0**), for after 2. . . . Qxe5, White gets a new queen by promoting his d-pawn. Without his bishop, Black has no counterattack whatsoever. Meanwhile, White's queen and rook will soon do a job on Black's king.

E. LOBRON VS. A. GREENFELD
ROGASKA SLATINA, YUGOSLAVIA, 1989

W: Ke3 Be6 Ps a2 d7 f6 g4 h2   (7)
B: Kf8 Rd6 Ps a6 b6 g6 h6   (6)

SHUT OFF
White to play and win

White has a slight material inferiority, bishop and pawn for a rook. Nevertheless, White can boast of two advanced pawns, at d7 and f6, which together with the bishop rope off the Black king, preventing its approach. Black's rook, positioned behind the most advanced pawn, prohibits safe promotion while also attacking the bishop, threatening to capture it with check.

After **1. Kf4**, Black resigned **(1-0)**. The bishop is immune to capture, for the rook must keep watching the d-file to stop the d-pawn's promotion.

White's winning technique is so simple. First he will place the king on e5, driving the rook back on the d-file. Then he will block the file by moving the bishop to d5 [*SHUT OFF*]. If Black tries a check from e1, White's king hides at d6.

P. Schlosser vs. M. Petursson
Munich, Germany, 1989

W: Kf3 Qb6 Ps a5 f2 g3 h4   (6)
B: Kg7 Rb2 Bf6 Ps f7 g6 h5   (6)

SIMPLIFICATION
White to play and win

Black angles to draw by posting his rook on the a-file and his bishop on the a7-f2 diagonal. Both pieces then converge on a7, preventing the a-pawn's advance.

This convergence is rendered impossible by **1. Qxb2!** [*SIMPLIFICATION*]. After **1. ... Bxb2**, Black probably planned to relocate his bishop to the a7-f2 diagonal. That idea was scotched by **2. Ke4** (technique), and Black resigned (**1-0**).

If Black tries 2. ... Ba3, heading for c5, White spoils that by **3. Kd5** (technique). The a-pawn would then be unstoppable (promotion).

P. POPOVIC VS. V. BAGIROV

MOSCOW, USSR, 1989
WORLD CUP QUALIFIER

W: Kg1 Bc8 Ps e5 g5 h2   (5)
B: Kf8 Ps b6 f6 g7 h7   (5)

TECHNIQUE
White to play and win

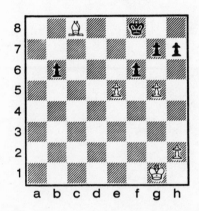

A winning plan can misfire if the technique is imperfect. How you do it makes all the difference.

White has a chance to win, but if he goes in for the straightforward 1. gxf6 gxf6 2. e6, Black draws with 2. . . . Ke7, when White's e-pawn is ineffectual and his king must contend with passed pawns on opposite sides of the board, at b6 and f6.

The correct idea is to reposition the bishop to a more pivotal square, **1. Bf5!** [*TECHNIQUE*]. That redeployment menaces the h-pawn as it seizes the b1-h7 diagonal—two accomplishments with one move.

A loser is 1. . . . g6, which fails to 2. Bxg6 hxg6 3. gxf6, and White's connected pawns decide. And if 1. . . . h6, then 2. gxf6 gxf6 3. e6 sets up a dominating position. White's king can position itself to escort the e-pawn.

In the actual game Black played 1. . . . Kf7, and after 2. Bxh7 fxg5 3. Bf5, called it quits (1-0).

J. R. KOCH VS. M. WILDER
CANNES, FRANCE, 1989
GRAND PRIX

W: Kh5 Qc8 Ps a3 g3 h4 (5)
B: Kg7 Qe4 Ps a4 c6 f6 g5 (6)

SIMPLIFICATION
Black to play and win

If it were White's turn, his venturesome king and active queen against Black's exposed king should guarantee a draw. It's Black's move, however, giving the story a different ending, beginning with **1. . . . Qe2+.**

If White blocks the check, 2. Qg4, then 2. . . . Qe8 is mate. So **2. g4** was forced. Black zapped with **2. . . . Qa2!,** which threatened 3. . . . Qf7 mate, and White was constrained to resign (**0-1**).

Even if White scratches out an escape hatch at h4 by 3. hxg5, Black still mates by 3. . . . Qh2++. So White has to trade queens, 3. Qd7+ Qf7+ [*SIMPLIFICATION*] 4. Qxf7+ Kxf7, which loses the resulting king and pawn endgame. He simply can't get back in time to overtake the c-pawn.

A sample variation is 5. hxg5 c5 6. gxf6 c4 7. g5 c3 8. g6+ Kxf6 9. Kh6 c2 10. g7 c1/Q+.

94

A. Dreev vs. E. Geller
MOSCOW, USSR, 1989
REGIONAL A TOURNAMENT

W: Kg1 Qd6 Ps a2 b3 c4 d5 g2 h2   (8)
B: Kg5 Qe4 Ps a5 e5 h7 h5   (6)

SIMPLIFICATION
White to play and win

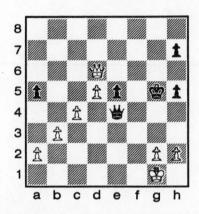

Make the queens magically disappear and White wins, thanks to his freewheeling connected passed pawns on the c- and d-files. In this case human craft and skill supplanted magic. White accomplished the trick by **1. h4 + !**. The trade of queens imminent, Black gave up **(1-0)**.

If Black plays 1. . . . Kf4, then 2. Qh6 + Kg3 (on either 2. . . . Kg4 or 2. . . . Kf5, mate is fashioned by 3. Qg5 + +) 3. Qg5 + Qg4 4. Qxg4 + [*SIMPLIFICA-TION*] and the d-pawn promotes.

If Black instead captures the h-pawn, 1. . . . Kxh4,

then 2. Qf6 + leads to a queen exchange next move by 3. Qf3 +, and again White subsequently queens the d-pawn.

As a final point, on 1. . . . Kg4, White simplifies by 2. Qe6 + Kg3 3. Qh3 + Kf4 4. Qf3 +, and makes a queen shortly.

95

I. BELOV VS. A. STRIKOVIC
PULA, YUGOSLAVIA, 1989

W: Kg2 Qf7 Bb6 Ps a5 e4 f2 g3 h3   (8)
B: Kc8 Qd8 Bc7 Ps c6 e5 f6 g6 h5   (8)

PROMOTION
White to play and win

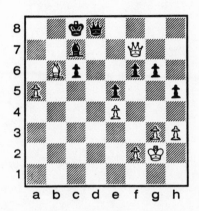

Materially, it's all tied up. Positionally, White has a big edge. His pieces are poised for kill, while Black's are defensively hunched. Moreover, White's king is safe, Black's is harried.

Waterloo came after **1. a6!** [*PROMOTION*]. Black resigned (**1-0**). Capturing White's b6-bishop, 1. . . . Bxb6, falls to 2. Qb7 mate, where the queen is anchored by the a-pawn.

An alternative defensive posture is 1. . . . Kb8, declining the b6-bishop. This fails to 2. a7+ Kb7 3. Qxc7+ (simplification) 3. . . . Qxc7 4. Bxc7, gaining a piece for White, since 4. . . . Kxc7 permits the a-pawn to queen.

Another debacle results from 1. . . . Qd7, offering

a queen trade. White accepts, 2. Qxd7+ Kxd7, and promotes by 3. a7. One more disaster ensues from 1. . . . Qd6. White wins by 2. Qe8+ Qd8 (or 2. . . . Bd8 3. Qxd8+ Qxd8 4. Bxd8, when 4. . . . Kxd8 loses to 5. a7) 3. Qxd8+ Bxd8 4. Bxd8, winning a piece, for Black can't take the bishop and then stop the pawn.

96

J. Fedorowicz vs. A. Ivanov

LONG BEACH, CA, USA, 1989
U.S. CHAMPIONSHIP, ROUND 2

W: Kh1 Rb1 Ba5 Bg2 Ne4 Ps d3 d5 g3 h2   (9)
B: Kg8 Re8 Bg7 Nc8 Nd4 Ps e5 f5 g6 h7   (9)

PROMOTION
White to play and win

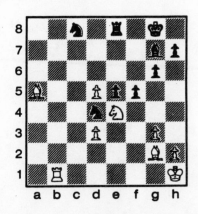

White's poor e4-knight is assailed by Black's f5-pawn. Wherever the knight moves, Black will be able to blockade White's d5-pawn by posting his c8-knight on d6. Rather than waste a critical tempo, White pushed his d5-pawn at once, **1. d6!** ("Passed pawns must be pushed!").

After **1. . . . fxe4,** White pressed on with **2. d7,** threatening to make a new queen [*PROMOTION*]. This forked Black's rook and c8-knight.

Black saved his rook, **2. . . . Rf8,** thinking to sacrifice it on d8 if necessary to stop the pawn. But White blew away this defense by **3. Rb8** (pin), when moving the c8-knight would allow a trade of rooks (removing the guard) and the promotion of the dangerous d-pawn. Black swung with **3. . . . Bf6,** but after **4. dxc8/ Q** threw in the towel **(1-0)**. Black winds up at least a rook behind.

97

I. STOHL VS. J. REYES
VRNJACKA BANJA, YUGOSLAVIA, 1989

W: Kg2 Rd1 Bd6 Ps b4 c6 e6 g3 h3   (8)
B: Kg8 Rc8 Bf8 Ps a6 b5 f6 g6 h7   (8)

PROMOTION
White to play and win

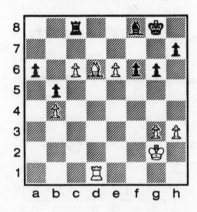

    White means business, with two far-advanced passed pawns. But let's not hurry. If he goes right for the jugular, 1. e7, then Black gives up his bishop for the two dangerous pawns, 1. . . . Bxe7 2. Bxe7 Rxc6, with some chances to mount resistance.

    Stronger is **1. c7!**, threatening 2. Bxf8 followed by 3. Rd8. Black shrewdly exchanged bishops, **1. . . . Bxd6 2. Rxd6,** hoping to gain the c-pawn by **2. . . . Rxc7,** but resigned after **3. Rd8 +** **(1-0).**

    On 3. . . . Kg7, White wins by 4. Rd7+ (fork) 4. . . . Rxd7 5. exd7 [*PROMOTION*], leading to a new queen at d8 next move.

98

V. KORCHNOI VS. G. KASPAROV

BARCELONA, SPAIN, 1989
WORLD CUP, ROUND 5

W: Kh2 Rc1 Ps d7 h4   (4)
B: Kf3 Ra8 Ps a2 f2   (4)

PROMOTION
Black to play and win

Two pawns about to queen for Black are undoubt-
edly an advantage over White's one pawn contender
for queenship. So is his option to move first, which
confers supreme advantage after **1. . . . a1/Q!** [*PRO-
MOTION*]. Overwhelmed by the force and simplicity
of this move, White resigned **(0-1)**.

Anyway, Black wins whether White captures the
new queen or promotes his own. If White promotes,
2. d8/Q, then the escape check, 2. . . . Qe5+, followed by 3. Kh1 (the sidestep 3. Kh3 is mated by 3. . . .
Qg3+ +) 3. . . . Rxd8 leaves Black well ahead.

If White captures the new queen at once, 2. Rxa1,
then 2. . . . Rxa1 3. d8/Q Rh1+! 4. Kxh1 f1/Q+ 5. Kh2
Qg2 is mate.

99

M. Petursson vs. A. Sherzer
PHILADELPHIA, PA, USA, 1989
WORLD OPEN

W: Kg1 Qc6 Ra1 Rf1 Ps a6 f2 g2 h2   (8)
B: Ke7 Qb2 Rd8 Nc3 Ps d2 e6 f7 g7 h7   (9)

PROMOTION
Black to play and win

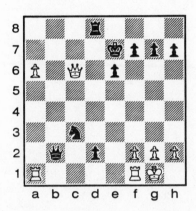

Perhaps it's irrelevant, but Black has the material disadvantage of a knight and pawn for a rook. Each side also boasts a menacing passed pawn, though Black's is a little more ominous, on its seventh rank, perched for promotion.

Black had better watch out, however. If he promotes immediately, 1. . . . d1/Q, he must contend with 2. Raxd1 Rxd1 (or 2. . . . Nxd1 3. a7) 3. Rxd1 Nxd1 4. Qb7+, trading queens and advancing a pawn to its eighth rank next move [*PROMOTION.*].

The correct idea is the reduction, 1. . . . Qxa1! (simplification), when 2. Rxa1 loses to 2. . . . d1/Q+ 3. Rxd1 Rxd1 mate. So White spurned the queen in favor of 2. Qc7+, but resigned after 2. . . . Rd7 (0-1).

If 3. Qxd7+ (or 3. Qc5+ Ke8 4. Qc8+ Rd8 5. Qc6+ Kf8 6. Qc5+ Kg8, and White has run out of checks) 3. . . . Kxd7 4. Rxa1, then 4. . . . Ne2+! (but not 4. . . . d1/Q+?, for 5. Rxd1 Nxd1 6. a7 leads to promotion) 5. Kf1 Nc1, shielding the promotion square, triumphs.

100

D. VELIMIROVIC VS. B. DAMJANOVIC
ZENICA, YUGOSLAVIA, 1989

W: Kf2 Rg1 Bg3 Ps a5 d3 h2   (6)
B: Kg8 Re8 Nd5 Ps a6 f7 f5 h7   (7)

SIMPLIFICATION
White to play and win

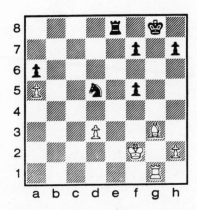

The rudiments: White has a bishop, Black a knight and an extra pawn, too, though it's doubled on the f-file. But the main attraction is the g-file. Here White can discover check to Black's king.

He did it by **1. Be5 +!** [discovery]. After the forced sidestep **1. . . . Kf8, 2. Bd6 + Ne7** followed, and White piled on the pinned knight, **3. Re1.** Clearing a space for the king, Black played **3. . . . f6.**

Black must unpin his king, giving White an extra move, which he used to improve his position, **4. Kf3.** He visualizes trading pieces and winning the king and pawn endgame by virtue of his better-placed king.

Black got out of the pin, **4. . . . Kf7,** but lost anyway

after 5. Bxe7 Rxe7 6. Rxe7+ [SIMPLIFICATION] 6. . . .
Kxe7 7. Kf4 Ke6 8. h4 h5 9. d4 Kd5 10. Kxf5 Kxd4
11. Kxf6. Here Black resigned (1-0).
A sample conclusion is 11. . . . Ke4 12. Kg5 Ke5
13. Kxh5 Kf5 14. Kh6 (book ending) 14. . . . Kf6 15. h5
Kf7 16. Kg5 Kg7 17. Kf5 Kh6 18. Ke5 Kxh5 19. Kd5 Kg5
20. Kc5 Kf5 21. Kb6 Ke6 22. Kxa6 Kd7 23. Kb7 and White
promotes.

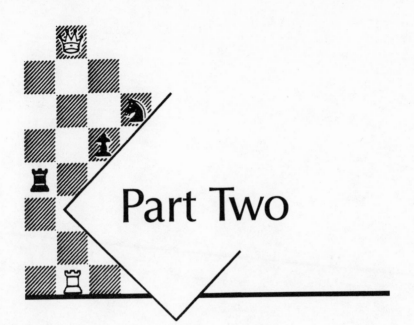

Part Two

Part Two

Little Chessercizes

1)	W: Kh2 Rg3 Bh1 Ph3	B: Ne2 Nh4 Pf4		(B)
2a)	W: Qe7 Ps g4 h4	B: Kh6 Ps g6 h7		(W)
2b)	W: Qe7 Rd8	B: Kg8 Ne8		(W)
2c)	W: Qe7 Rd8	B: Kh8 Ng8 Ph7		(W)
3)	W: Kg1 Pg2	B: Qd2 Rb2		(B)
4a)	W: Kg3 Bg1	B: Qf1 Rh2 Ph5		(B)
4b)	W: Kh3 Rc3 Ph4	B: Qf1 Rg2 Ng4		(B)
5a)	W: Qe7	B: Kh8 Ph7		(W)
5b)	W: Qf8 Pg4	B: Kh6 Qg7 Ps g6 h7		(W)
5c)	W: Kh3 Pg3	B: Qe3 Bf4		(B)
5d)	W: Kg5 Ps g4 h4	B: Qf2 Ps e7 g6 h7		(B)
5e)	W: Kd5	B: Qf6 Nd2 Pe7		(B)
6a)	W: Qc5 Rc8	B: Kd7 Pe6		(W)
6b)	W: Kd4 Qc5 Pe5	B: Qe2 Pd5		(B)
6c)	W: Kf3 Ne2 Pf4	B: Qd1 Rg2		(B)
6d)	W: Kf2 Ne2	B: Qh3 Rh1		(B)
7a)	W: Qf7 Nh6	B: Kh8		(W)
7b)	W: Qh5 Rh3	B: Kg8 Qb2 Rf8		(W)
8a)	W: Kh4 Rb7 Rf7	B: Kh6 Pg6		(W)
8b)	W: Rh7 Rb7 Bc5	B: Kg8		(W)
9a)	W: Pe7	B: Kg8 Rd8 Ps f7 g7 h7		(W)
9b)	W: Qe4	B: Kg8 Re8 Ps f6 g7 h7		(W)
9c)	W: Kg1 Qe1 Pg2	B: Qh4 Rd1		(B)
10a)	W: Kh4 Rb7 Rh7 Ps d4 g4	B: Kf6 Re3		(W)
10b)	W: Kh4 Rh6 Re7	B: Kf4 Rd4 Re3		(W)
10c)	W: Rf7 Rh7 Pg4	B: Kg6 Ph6		(W)
10d)	W: Kh4 Rf7 Rg7 Pg4	B: Kh6 Ph5		(W)
11a)	W: Kh6	B: Kg8 Rf5 Ps g6 h7		(B)
11b)	W: Kg4 Nf3 Ph3	B: Qf2 Rf5 Ps g6 h7		(B)
11c)	W: Kh6 Nh4	B: Kg8 Qg3 Ps g6 h7		(B)
12a)	W: Rg3 Rh7 Bc1	B: Kh5 Qh6		(W)
12b)	W: Rg3 Rf7	B: Kh5		(W)
12c)	W: Kh2 Rg3	B: Qd6 Ph4		(B)
13a)	W: Ke1 Ng1	B: Rf2 Rh1 Pg3		(B)
13b)	W: Rb8 Ba4 Pe5	B: Ke7 Pf7		(W)
13c)	W: Rb7	B: Kf8 Ne7 Ps f7 g7		(W)
14a)	W: Qg5 Nd6 Pe5	B: Kd7 Rd8 Bc6 Pe6		(W)
14b)	W: Qf5 Nd6 Pe5	B: Ke7 Rd8		(W)
14c)	W: Qf5 Rd3 Ps a2 b2	B: Kb4		(W)
14d)	W: Qd5 Rd3 Nd6	B: Kb4		(W)
15a)	W: Rh8 Bg4	B: Kg6 Rf7		(W)
15b)	W: Rd5 Rh8 Bg4 Pg5	B: Kg6 Pg7		(W)
16a)	W: Rd1 Nc3	B: Ke5 Na5		(W)
16b)	W: Rd5 Rf1 Ne4 Nc3 Pd6	B: Ke6		(W)
17a)	W: Qb4 Bh4	B: Ke8		(W)
17b)	W: Qf8 Na6	B: Kd7 Ps c7 c6		(W)
18a)	W: Qe3 Rb1 Bc5 Pd4	B: Kc4 Qd5 Pc3		(W)
18b)	W: Kg1	B: Qf3 Bb7		(B)
18c)	W: Qe3 Rb4 Pd4	B: Kd5 Qc6		(W)

19a)	W: Kf4 Pf3	B: Qh5 Ps d5 h6	(B)
19b)	W: Kf4 Ne6	B: Kg6 Qh5	(B)
19c)	W: Kf4 Be5 Pg4	B: Qh5 Ps d5 h6	(B)
20a)	W: Qf4 Rd3	B: Kh3 Qg3	(W)
20b)	W: Qh2 Rd4 Ne6	B: Kh4 Qh3 Be4 Ph5	(W)
21a)	W: Qb7 Rh6 Bc4	B: Kc5 Pd4	(W)
21b)	W: Qg7 Pf2	B: Kf4 Rf5 Pe4	(W)
21c)	W: Qb7 Rh7 Bc4	B: Kd6 Qd8	(W)
21d)	W: Qg5 Rh6 Bc4	B: Ke5 Rf5 Pd4	(W)
22a)	W: Kg4 Ps f4 g3	B: Qh1 Pg6	(B)
22b)	W: Kf4 Nd2 Ps f5 e4 g3	B: Qh5 Rc3 Ps d6 g6	(B)
23a)	W: Kh2 Ph3	B: Qg5 Re1 Pg2	(B)
23b)	W: Qf3 Rb7	B: Ka6 Pa5	(W)
23c)	W: Qf3 Rc7	B: Kd6 Re5	(W)
23d)	W: Qf3 Rc7 Pb3	B: Kd4 Re5	(W)
23e)	W: Qf3 Rc7	B: Kb6 Pa5	(W)
24a)	W: Kf3 Pf4	B: Qg1 Bh4 Pf5	(B)
24b)	W: Kf5 Qd3	B: Kg7 Qg1	(B)
24c)	W: Ke6 Qd5	B: Qc5 Bf6 Pg6	(B)
24d)	W: Ke5 Pf4	B: Qc6 Bh4 Pg6	(B)
24e)	W: Kd5 Qd6	B: Qe7 Ps f5 b6	(B)
25a)	W: Rc7 Ne6 Pf6	B: Ke8	(W)
25b)	W: Rc7 Ne6	B: Kg8 Nf7 Ph7	(W)
26a)	W: Kb4 Qb5	B: Rh2	(B)
26b)	W: Ke3 Pe4	B: Qh1 Rh2 Ps g4 e5	(B)
26c)	W: Kg2	B: Qe3 Rh1 Pg4	(B)
27a)	W: Qg7 Re6	B: Kh5	(W)
27b)	W: Kg2 Qh7 Pg3	B: Kg4 Qc1 Pf5	(W)
27c)	W: Kg2 Qh7 Re6 Pg3	B: Kg5 Qc1 Pf5	(W)
28a)	W: Kh3 Nh2 Pg3	B: Qa2 Rc2 Ph5	(B)
28b)	W: Kg3 Pg4	B: Qa2 Rh2	(B)
28c)	W: Kh4 Qg5 Pg4	B: Qc2 Rf3	(B)
28d)	W: Kd4 Re5	B: Qc2 Re3 Pb6	(B)
29)	W: Rc8 Re4 Bf5 Bf4	B: Kd7 Qe6 Be7	(W)
30a)	W: Kf1	B: Qe3 Bg4	(B)
30b)	W: Kf1	B: Qg3 Bf5	(B)
30c)	W: Kd1 Rc1	B: Qf2 Bf5	(B)
30d)	W: Kg1 Rc1	B: Qe2	(B)
30e)	W: Kc3 Rc1 Pb2	B: Qf2 Bf5	(B)
31a)	W: Ka1 Nb1 Pa2	B: Qd1 Rc1	(B)
31b)	W: Ka1 Nb1 Pa2	B: Rc1 Be7	(B)
31c)	W: Ka1 Nb1 Nd2 Pa2	B: Qc2 Rc1	(B)
31d)	W: Ka1 Nb1 Nd2	B: Qd1 Rc1	(B)
32)	W: Rf7 Rf8	B: Kh6 Qg5 Pg6	(W)
33a)	W: Qg6 Be4	B: Kh8	(W)
33b)	W: Qg6 Re8	B: Kh8 Qf8	(W)
34a)	W: Qb3 Bd6	B: Ke8 Bd7	(W)
34b)	W: Qf7 Be5	B: Kh8 Pg7	(W)
35a)	W: Kh1 Qg1	B: Qh4 Rf2 Bh3	(B)
35b)	W: Kh1 Qh2	B: Qh3 Rf2	(B)
35c)	W: Kg1	B: Qh4 Ra2 Bg2	(B)
36a)	W: Kc1 Qd2	B: Qb3 Ra3	(B)
36b)	W: Kb1 Qb2	B: Qc4 Rc3	(B)
36c)	W: Ka2 Qb2	B: Qd3 Rc3	(B)

36d)	W: Ka1 Qb2	B: Qc4 Rc3	(B)
37a)	W: Kh1	B: Kg3 Re5	(B)
37b)	W: Kg1	B: Kg3 Rh5 Bg2	(B)
37c)	W: Kf1	B: Kg3 Rh5 Bf3	(B)
38a)	W: Kg1 Bg2	B: Qa2 Rb2	(B)
38b)	W: Qh8 Rc8 Pd5	B: Kf7 Re7 Nd7 Pf6	(W)
38c)	W: Qh6 Rc8 Pd5	B: Kf7 Re7 Nf8 Pf6	(W)
38d)	W: Qh6 Rc8	B: Kg8 Nf8	(W)
38e)	W: Qh8 Rg8 Pd5	B: Kf7 Re7 Nd7 Pf6	(W)
38f)	W: Qh8 Rg8 Pe4	B: Kg6 Rg7 Pf6	(W)
39a)	W: Rh4 Bg7 Pf6	B: Kg8 Pf7	(W)
39b)	W: Qh6 Bg7	B: Kg8 Pf7	(W)
40a)	W: Kh1 Bg2 Ps g3 h2	B: Bd5 Ne1 Pf2	(B)
40b)	W: Kh1 Qf1 Ps g3 h2	B: Qh3	(B)
41a)	W: Qe7 Bh6	B: Kg8 Rd8 Ps f7 h7	(W)
41b)	W: Rd8 Bh6	B: Kg8 Re8 Ps f7 h7	(W)
41c)	W: Qf7 Bc4 Bh6	B: Kh8 Qc8 Ph7	(W)
41d)	W: Qe7 Bf7 Bh6	B: Kh8 Qc8 Ph7	(W)
42a)	W: Kg1 Bf1 Pg2	B: Qh4 Bg3	(B)
42b)	W: Kh1 Bf1	B: Qe1 Ng4	(B)
43a)	W: Kg1 Pg2	B: Qg3 Rf2	(B)
43b)	W: Kf1	B: Qg3 Rg2	(B)
43c)	W: Kh1	B: Qg3 Rg2	(B)
44a)	W: Kh1 Qc1 Ph2	B: Qf2 Bd4	(B)
44b)	W: Kh4 Pg3	B: Qf3 Pg6	(B)
44c)	W: Kg4 Pg3	B: Qh2 Ps g6 e5	(B)
44d)	W: Kh3 Pg3	B: Qf2 Nf3 Ph5	(B)
45a)	W: Qa7 Ne5	B: Kc8 Pc7	(W)
45b)	W: Qd7 Rf1 Pc3	B: Ke4	(W)
45c)	W: Qd4 Re2 Rf1	B: Ke6 Be4	(W)
45d)	W: Qc7 Rf2 Nf7	B: Ke6 Qf8 Bd5	(W)
45e)	W: Qc7 Rf2 Nf7	B: Ke6	(W)
45f)	W: Qa7 Rf7	B: Kc8 Pb7	(W)
46a)	W: Qe7 Rd7	B: Kg8 Qb1 Rf8	(W)
46b)	W: Qe7 Rd7	B: Kg8 Qg5 Rf8	(W)
46c)	W: Qh8 Rh5	B: Kg6 Rf7	(W)
47a)	W: Kg1 Qe2	B: Qb7 Rf8 Ba8	(B)
47b)	W: Kh1 Ps h2 g3	B: Rg2 Ba8	(B)
48a)	W: Rd7 Re1	B: Kf7 Rb8 Bb7 Be7	(W)
48b)	W: Rc7 Re1	B: Kf7 Qd7 Rb8 Bb7 Be7	(W)
48c)	W: Qb8 Rc1	B: Qd7 Bb7	(W)
49)	W: Kg1	B: Kf3 Rh6 Pg2	(B)
50a)	W: Rc8 Bb5 Pe5	B: Ke7 Pf7	(W)
50b)	W: Kg3 Rh8 Pe5	B: Bd4	(B)
51a)	W: Kf6 Qe4	B: Kh6	(W)
51b)	W: Kf6 Qh1	B: Kg8 Ra7	(W)
51c)	W: Kf6 Qg4	B: Kf8	(W)
51d)	W: Kf6 Qh2	B: Kh8 Rh7	(W)
51e)	W: Kf6 Qh2	B: Kg8 Ra7	(W)
51f)	W: Kf6 Qa7	B: Kh8	(W)
51g)	W: Kf6 Qg7	B: Kh5	(W)
51h)	W: Kf6 Qh1	B: Kh8 Rh7	(W)
52a)	W: Kg1 Qc1 Nd4 Pc3	B: Qh4 Rc8	(B)
52b)	W: Ke3 Qc1	B: Qh4	(B)

	W:	B:	
52c)	Kg1 Qc1 Ps g2 h2	Qg5 Rf2 Rf8	(B)
52d)	Kg1 Ps g2 h2	Rf8 Rf2	(B)
53a)	Qb7 Pf3	Kg6 Nf2	(W)
53b)	Qa8 Ps a2 f3	Kf7 Nf2	(W)
54a)	Kg3 Qf8 Ps g4 h3	Kg5 Re4 Pg6	(W)
54b)	Qf8 Pg4	Kh6 Rg7 Ps g6 h7	(W)
54c)	Qd8 Bh6	Kg8 Re8 Ps f7 h7	(W)
55a)	Ne4	Kg8 Re8	(W)
55b)	Ne4 Pf5	Kg7 Re7	(W)
55c)	Ne4	Kf7 Re8	(W)
55d)	Rd8 Ne6	Kh8 Re8 Ph7	(W)
55e)	Nf6	Kh6 Re7	(W)
56a)	Qe7 Ph6	Kg8	(W)
56b)	Qf6 Be2	Kh5 Qf3	(W)
56c)	Kh2 Qg7 Be2 Ph6	Kh4 Pf5	(W)
56d)	Qf6 Bf5	Kg8 Qd5	(W)
57a)	Ka1 Qc1 Ps a2 b2	Rc8	(B)
57b)	Qg1 Nf5	Kh7 Rg7	(W)
57c)	Ka1 Qb1 Pb2	Rc1 Be4 Pb3	(B)
58a)	Kg2 Rb1	Qa4	(B)
58b)	Kf3 Pg4	Qa4 Pg5	(B)
59a)	Kh2 Ng3 Pg2	Qd8	(B)
59b)	Qg8 Pf4	Kf6 Ps e6 f7	(W)
60a)	Qh7	Kf7 Rf8 Bg7 Pg6	(B)
60b)	Qg6 Bd4	Kf8	(W)
60c)	Qh7 Rg6 Bd4	Kf7 Qa6 Rg8 Bg7 Pf6	(W)
61a)	Re1 Rc1 Bc7 Nd5	Kd7	(W)
61b)	Rc1 Bc7 Nd5	Kc8 Pb7	(W)
61c)	Rc1 Re1 Nd5 Nf7	Kd7 Re8 Be7 Pc7	(W)
62)	Qc7 Rd1 Bf1	Qa6 Rb8 Rd8 Bd3	(W)
63a)	Kh1 Ph2	Rg8 Ng4	(B)
63b)	Rf1 Bb3	Kf7 Re6 Nf6	(W)
63c)	Bb3 Pd6	Kf7 Re6 Pc7	(W)
64)	Qc4 Bb3	Qb6 Bd7 Pf7	(B)
65a)	Qb1 Re1	Kg8 Re8 Be2 Ps d3 f7 g7 h7	(W)
65b)	Qd1 Bf1	Kg8 Re2 Ps d3 f7 g7 h7	(W)
65c)	Qd1	Kg8 Ps e2 f7 g7 h7	(W)
66a)	Kg1 Rd8 Pf2	Ps e3 e6	(B)
66b)	Kh1 Re1	Rd8 Pe2	(B)
67a)	Re2 Pf2	Re8 Be5	(W)
67b)	Qd5 Re1	Qd7 Be5 Pd6	(W)
67c)	Qd5 Re1	Kg8 Qf7 Re8	(W)
68a)	Kd3 Rd4 Be3	Qb2 Rg2	(B)
68b)	Kc2 Qe4 Rf5 Rd2 Be3	Qe2 Bg4	(B)
68c)	Kc2 Qe4 Rd4 Rf5 Bd2	Qe2 Bg4	(B)
69)	Rh8	Ke7 Rb7	(W)
70a)	Kd2 Qa4	Rd8 Nd3	(B)
70b)	Kd2 Nc3	Rd8 Re8 Ba4 Nd3 Nh4	(B)
71)	Kf3 Re6 Ne4	Kf7 Re2 Rh2	(W)
72a)	Qc8	Kg6 Be4	(W)
72b)	Qc8	Ke5 Qg7	(W)
73a)	Qd2 Be2 Be3 Nc3	Be5 Nf4	(B)
73b)	Qd2 Rb1	Bg6 Pe4	(B)
73c)	Qd2 Rb1 Nc3	Be5 Bg6	(B)

73d)	W: Qc3 Kg2	B: Bb1 Pb2	(B)
73e)	W: Qc3 Rf4 Be3	B: Kg8 Qf7 Re8 Rf8 Pg7	(B)
74a)	W: Kf4 Qf1	B: Qc8	(B)
74b)	W: Ke3 Qd2	B: Qb1 Ba3	(B)
74c)	W: Kh7 Bg7	B: Qf7 Rf6 Bc1	(B)
75)	W: Rg6 Be6	B: Kf8 Qe7	(W)
76a)	W: Qc3 Bb2	B: Kg8 Rd8 Bc5 Ps f7 g6	(B)
76b)	W: Qc3 Bb2 Bc4	B: Kg8 Pf7	(W)
76c)	W: Qf3 Bb2 Bc4	B: Kg8 Pf7	(W)
77a)	W: Kd1 Ra2	B: Ne4	(B)
77b)	W: Ra7 Nf7	B: Rb3 Pa2	(B)
78a)	W: Ba7	B: Kc8 Ps c5 d6 e7	(B)
78b)	W: Kf2 Ra1 Ba7	B: Kb7 Bd3 Bd2 Pe2	(B)
79a)	W: Qc2 Rc8 Ne4	B: Kh7 Ps g7 h6	(W)
79b)	W: Qc2 Rh8	B: Kg7 Qg6	(W)
80a)	W: Rb8 Bd5	B: Kh8 Rg8 Ph7	(W)
80b)	W: Qg3	B: Kh8 Rb8 Pe5	(W)
80c)	W: Qb8	B: Kh8 Bf8 Ph7	(W)
81a)	W: Ka2	B: Rd1 Be5 Pa4	(B)
81b)	W: Ka2 Rb1 Pa3	B: Rd1 Be5 Pa4	(B)
81c)	W: Ka2 Rb2 Pa3	B: Rc2 Rd1 Be5 Pa4	(B)
82a)	W: Kg1 Nc5 Nc3 Ps a6 b3	B: Kf4 Bf7 Nb4	(B)
82b)	W: Kg1 Nd5 Pa6	B: Ke5 Be8 Pg6	(W)
82c)	W: Nd5	B: Kf5 Bc6	(W)
83a)	W: Kh1 Rd1 Bf3 Ps g3 h2	B: Qh3 Ra2	(B)
83b)	W: Kh1 Rb1 Ps g3 h2	B: Qh3 Rh6	(B)
83c)	W: Kh1 Qf3 Ph2	B: Bc5 Be4	(B)
83d)	W: Kh1 Ph2	B: Qh3	(B)
83e)	W: Kh1 Qf3 Ph2	B: Qh3 Bc5	(B)
84a)	W: Rf7 Nd5 Pc4	B: Kc6 Pd6	(W)
84b)	W: Rf7 Nd5 Pe4	B: Ke6 Pd6	(W)
84c)	W: Nd5	B: Kd7 Rg8	(W)
85a)	W: Rf1	B: Kh8 Rf8 Ng7 Ph7	(W)
85b)	W: Qf5 Bd4 Be8	B: Kg8 Qf7	(W)
86a)	W: Kg1 Qe8 Be4	B: Kh8 Qd4 Rf2	(B)
86b)	W: Kh2	B: Qc1 Rg3	(B)
86c)	W: Kg2 Rf2 Pg3	B: Qc1 Rh7	(B)
87a)	W: Kh4 Rf2	B: Ba5 Pd3	(B)
87b)	W: Rc4	B: Ps c5 d3	(B)
88a)	W: Qc8 Bd5	B: Kh8 Rg8 Ph7	(W)
88b)	W: Qg5 Bd5	B: Kh8	(W)
88c)	W: Qh6 Be4 Bb4	B: Kg8 Rd8	(W)
89)	W: Kh1	B: Qf4 Be5	(B)
90a)	W: Ke5 Be6 Ps d7 f6	B: Rd1 Kf8	(W)
90b)	W: Ke5 Bd5 Ps d7 f6	B: Re1 Kf8	(W)
91a)	W: Pa6	B: Bb2	(B)
91b)	W: Pa6	B: Ba3	(B)
91c)	W: Kf3 Ps a5 f2	B: Bb2	(W)
91d)	W: Ke4 Ps a5 f2	B: Ba3	(W)
91e)	W: Qb7 Pa6	B: Ra2 Bf6	(B)
92)	W: Kh1 Bf5 Pe5	B: Ke7 Pf6	(W)
93a)	W: Kh5 Qg4 Ph4	B: Kg7 Qe2 Ps f6 g5	(B)
93b)	W: Kh5 Ps g5 g4	B: Kg7 Qa2	(B)
94a)	W: Qh6 Ps d5 h4	B: Kf5 Qe4	(W)

94b)	W:	Qh6 Ps g2 h4	B: Kg4	(W)
95a)	W:	Qf7 Pa6	B: Kc8 Qd8	(W)
95b)	W:	Pa6	B: Kd8	(W)
96a)	W:	Pd6	B: Re8 Nc8	(W)
96b)	W:	Rb1 Pd7	B: Rf8 Nc8	(W)
97a)	W:	Rd8 Pe6	B: Kg7 Rc7	(W)
97b)	W:	Rd1 Pc7	B: Kg8 Rf8	(W)
97c)	W:	Rd1 Pc7	B: Kf8 Rc8	(W)
98a)	W:	Kh3 Ph4	B: Kf3 Qe5	(B)
98b)	W:	Kh2	B: Kf3 Qf1	(B)
99a)	W:	Kg1 Ps f2 g2 h2	B: Rd8	(B)
99b)	W:	Qc6 Pa6	B: Ke7 Qb2	(W)
99c)	W:	Kf1 Ra1	B: Ne2 Pd2	(B)
100a)	W:	Ka6 Pa5	B: Kd7	(W)
100b)	W:	Ka6 Pa5	B: Kd7	(B)

Little Answers

1)   Black mates by
       1. . . . fxg3 ++
2a)   White mates by 1. Qf8 ++
2b)   White mates by 1. Rxe8 ++
2c)   White mates by 1. Qf6 ++
       or 1. Qe5 ++
3)   Black mates by
       1. . . . Qxg2 ++
4a)   Black mates by 1. . . . Rh3 ++
4b)   Black mates by 1. . . . Rg1 ++
5a)   White mates by 1. Qf8 ++
5b)   White drives off the
       defender by 1. g5 +
5c)   Black mates by
       1. . . . Qxg3 ++
5d)   Black mates by
       1. . . . Qe3 ++
       or 1. . . . Qd2 ++
5e)   Black mates by
       1. . . . Qd6 ++
6a)   White mates by 1. Qc7 ++
6b)   Black mates by
       1. . . . Qd2 ++
6c)   Black mates by
       1. . . . Qxe2 ++
6d)   Black mates by 1. . . . Rf1 ++
7a)   White mates by 1. Qg8 ++
7b)   White mates by 1. Qh7 ++
8a)   White mates by 1. Rh7 ++
8b)   White mates by 1. Rbg7 ++
9a)   White mates by 1. exd8/Q ++
       or 1. exd8/R ++
9b)   White mates by 1. Qxe8 ++
9c)   Black mates by
       1. . . . Rxe1 ++
10a) White mates by 1. Rh6 ++
10b) White mates by 1. Rf6 ++
10c) White mates by 1. Rhg7 ++
10d) White mates by 1. g5 ++
11a) Black mates by 1. . . . Rh5 ++
11b) Black mates by 1. . . . h5 ++
11c) Black mates by 1. . . . Qxh4 ++
       or 1. . . . Qf4 ++
       or 1. . . . Qe3 ++
12a) White mates by 1. Rxh6 ++
12b) White mates by 1. Rh7 ++

12c) Black gains a rook by
       1. . . . Qxg3 +
       or 1. . . . hxg3 +
13a) Black mates by
       1. . . . Rxg1 ++
13b) White mates by 1. Re8 ++
13c) White wins a knight by
       1. Rb8 +
14a) White mates by 1. Qg7 ++
14b) White mates by 1. Qxf7 ++
14c) White mates by 1. Rd4 ++
14d) White mates by 1. Qb5 ++
15a) White skewers by 1. Bh5 +
15b) White mates by Bh5 ++
16a) White forks by 1. Rd5 +
16b) White mates by 1. Nc5 ++
17a) White mates by 1. Qe7 ++
17b) White mates by 1. Nc5 ++
18a) White mates by 1. Rb4 ++
       or 1. Qe2 ++
18b) Black mates by
       1. . . . Qg2 ++
18c) White mates by 1. Qe5 ++
19a) Black mates by
       1. . . . Qg5 ++
19b) Black forks by 1. . . . Qf5 +
19c) Black deflects the king by
       1. . . . Qg5 +
20a) White mates by 1. Qxg3 ++
20b) White mates by 1. Rxe4 ++
21a) White mates by 1. Qb5 ++
       or 1. Rc6 ++
21b) White mates by 1. Qg3 ++
21c) White mates by 1. Qd5 ++
21d) White mates by 1. Re6 ++
22a) Black mates by
       1. . . . Qh5 ++
22b) Black mates by 1. . . . g5 ++
23a) Black mates by 1. . . . Rh1 ++
       or 1. . . . g1/Q ++
23b) White mates by 1. Qc6 ++
23c) White mates by 1. Qc6 ++
23d) White mates by 1. Rc4 ++
23e) White mates by 1. Qc6 ++
       or 1. Qb7 ++
24a) Black mates by 1. . . . Qf2 ++

24b) Black skewers by
1. . . . *Qg6+*

24c) Black mates by
1. . . . *Qe7++*

24d) Black mates by 1. . . . *Bf6++*

24e) Black mates by
1. . . . *Qe4++*

25a) White mates by 1. *Re7++*

25b) White wins a knight by
1. *Rc8+*

26a) Black skewers by
1. . . . *Rb2+*

26b) Black mates by 1. . . . *Qf3++*

26c) Black mates by 1. . . . *Qf3++*
or 1. . . .*Qg1++*

27a) White mates by 1. *Rh6++*

27b) White mates by 1. *Qh4++*

27c) White mates by 1. *Qh4++*
or 1. *Rg6++*
or 1. *Qg6++*

28a) Black mates by
1. . . . *Rxh2++*

28b) Black mates by 1. . . . *Qf2++*

28c) Black mates by
1. . . . *Qh2++*

28d) Black mates by
1. . . . *Qd3++*

29) White mates by 1. *Bxe6++*

30a) Black mates by 1. . . . *Bh3++*

30b) Black mates by 1. . . . *Bd3++*

30c) Black mates by 1. . . . *Bg4++*

30d) Black forks by 1. . . . *Qe3+*

30e) Black forks by 1. . . . *Qe3+*

31a) Black mates by
1. . . . *Rxb1++*

31b) Black mates by 1. . . . *Bf6++*

31c) Black mates by
1. . . . *Qc3++*

31d) Black exploits the pin by
1. . . . *Qxd2*

32) White mates by 1. *Rh8++*

33a) White mates by 1. *Qh7++*

33b) White mates by 1. *Rxf8++*

34a) White mates by 1. *Qg8++*

34b) White mates by 1. *Qxg7++*

35a) Black mates by 1. . . . *Bg2++*

35b) Black mates by
1. . . . *Qxh2++*
or 1. . . . *Rf1++*

35c) Black mates by
1. . . . *Qh1++*

36a) Black mates by 1. . . . *Ra1++*

36b) Black pins by 1. . . . *Rb3*

36c) Black pins by 1. . . . *Rc2*

36d) Black wins the queen by
1. . . . *Rc1+*

37a) Black mates by 1. . . . *Re1++*

37b) Black mates by 1. . . . *Rh1++*

37c) Black mates by 1. . . . *Rh1++*

38a) Black forces mate by
1. . . . *Rxg2+*

38b) White mates by 1. *Qh7++*
or 1. *Qg8++*

38c) White mates by 1. *Rxf8++*

38d) White mates by 1. *Rxf8++*

38e) White mates by 1. *Rg7++*
or 1. *Qg7++*
or 1. *Qh7++*

38f) White mates by 1. *Rxg7++*

39a) White mates by 1. *Rh8++*

39b) White mates by 1. *Qh8++*

40a) Black mates by
1. . . . *Bxg2++*
or 1. . . . *f1/Q++*
or 1. . . . *f1/R++*

40b) Black mates by
1. . . . *Qxf1++*

41a) White mates by 1. *Qxd8++*

41b) White mates by 1. *Rxe8++*

41c) White mates by 1. *Qg7++*
or 1. *Qf6++*
or 1. *Bg7++*

41d) White mates by 1. *Qf6++*
or 1. *Qe5++*

42a) Black mates by
1. . . . *Qh2++*
or 1. . . . *Bf2++*

42b) Black mates by
1. . . . *Qxf1++*

43a) Black mates by
1. . . . *Qxg2++*

43b) Black mates by
1. . . . *Qf2++*

43c) Black mates by
1. . . . *Qh2++*
or 1. . . . *Qh3++*
or 1. . . . *Rh2++*
or 1. . . . *Rg1++*

44a) Black mates by 1. . . . *Qf3++*

44b) Black mates by
1. . . . *Qh5++*

44c) Black mates by
1. . . . *Qh5++*

44d) Black mates by
1. . . . *Qh2++*

45a) White mates by 1. *Qa8++*

45b) White mates by 1. *Qd4++*

45c) White mates by 1. *Rxe4++*

45d)	White mates by *1. Ng5*++	**57a)**	Black mates by
45e)	White mates by *1. Qd6*++		*1. . . . Rxc1*++
45f)	White mates by *1. Qa8*++	**57b)**	White mates by *1. Qxg7*++
46a)	White mates by *1. Qg7*++	**57c)**	Black mates by
46b)	White mates by *1. Qh7*++		*1. . . . Rxb1*++
46c)	White mates by *1. Qh6*++	**58a)**	Black forks by *1. . . . Qe4*+
47a)	Black mates by		or *1. . . . Qa2*+
	1. . . . Qh1++		or *1. . . . Qc2*+
47b)	Black mates by	**58b)**	Black wins the g-pawn by
	1. . . . Rxg3++		*1. . . . Qf4*+
48a)	White forks by *1. Rexe7*+	**59a)**	Black wins a knight by
48b)	White forks and pins by		*1. . . . Qh4*+
	1. Rxd7	**59b)**	White mates by *1. Qg5*++
48c)	White forks by *1. Rc7*	**60a)**	Black traps the queen by
49)	Black mates by *1. . . . Rh1*++		*1. . . . Rh8*
50a)	White mates by *1. Re8*++	**60b)**	White mates by *1. Bc5*++
50b)	Black forks by *1. . . . Bxe5*+	**60c)**	White exploits the pin by
51a)	White mates by *1. Qh1*++		*1. Rxf6*+
	or *1. Qg6*++	**61a)**	White mates by *1. Nb6*++
	or *1. Qh4*++	**61b)**	White mates by *1. Nb6*++
51b)	White forks by *1. Qg1*+	**61c)**	White mates by *1. Rxc7*++
51c)	White mates by *1. Qc8*++	**62)**	White exploits the overload
51d)	White mates by *1. Qb8*++		by *1. Bxd3*
51e)	White forks by *1. Qb8*+		or *1. Rxd3*
	or *1. Qg1*+	**63a)**	Black mates by *1. . . . Nf2*++
51f)	White mates by *1. Qg7*++	**63b)**	White piles on the pinned
51g)	White mates by *1. Qg5*++		rook by *1. Re1*
51h)	White mates by *1. Qa8*++	**63c)**	White wins a pawn by
52a)	Black exploits the pin by		*1. dxc7* and soon
	1. . . . Qxd4+		promotes
52b)	Black skewers by	**64)**	Black skewers by *1. . . . Be6*
	1. . . . Qg5+	**65a)**	White exploits the pin by
	or *1. . . . Qh6*+		*1. Qxd3*
52c)	Black mates by	**65b)**	White exploits the pin by
	1. . . . Qxg2++		*1. Bxe2*
	or *1. . . . Qxc1*++	**65c)**	White mates by *1. Qd8*++
52d)	Black mates by *1. . . . Rf1*++	**66a)**	Black promotes by *1. . . . e2*
53a)	White forks by *1. Qb6*+	**66b)**	Black pins by *1. . . . Rd1*
53b)	White forks by *1. Qa7*+	**67a)**	White exploits the pin by
54a)	White mates by *1. h4*++		*1. f4*
54b)	White deflects by *1. g5*+	**67b)**	White exploits the pin by
54c)	White mates by *1. Qxe8*++		*1. Rxe5*
55a)	White forks by *1. Nf6*+	**67c)**	White exploits the pin by
55b)	White forks by *1. f6*+		*1. Rxe8*+
55c)	White forks by *1. Nd6*+	**68a)**	Black mates by
55d)	White mates by *1. Rxe8*++		*1. . . . Qc2*++
55e)	White forks by *1. Ng8*+	**68b)**	Black deflects by *1. . . . Bxf5*
56a)	White mates by *1. Qg7*++	**68c)**	Black removes the guard by
56b)	White mates by *1. Bxf3*++		*1. . . . Qxe4*+
56c)	White mates by *1. Qg3*++	**69)**	White skewers by *1. Rh7*+
	or *1. Qf6*++	**70a)**	Black discovers by
	or *1. Qe7*++		*1. . . . Nc5*+
56d)	White forks by *1. Be6*+		or *1. . . . Nb2*+

70b)	Black mates by *1. . . . Nf3* ++
71)	White discovers by *1. Ng5* +
72a)	White forks by *1. Qe6* +
72b)	White skewers by *1. Qc3* +
73a)	Black removes the guard by *1. . . . Bxc3*
73b)	Black discovers by *1. . . . e3*
73c)	Black removes the guard by *1. . . . Bxc3*
73d)	Black promotes by *1. . . . Be4* +
73e)	Black removes the guard by *1. . . . Rxe3*
74a)	Black skewers by *1. . . . Qf8* +
74b)	Black pins by *1. . . . Bc1*
74c)	Black mates by *1. . . . Rh6* ++
75)	White mates by *1. Rg8* ++
76a)	Black defends the long diagonal by *1. . . . Bd4*
76b)	White mates by *1. Qg7* ++ or *1. Qh8* ++
76c)	White mates by *1. Qxf7* ++
77a)	Black forks by *1. . . . Nc3* +
77b)	Black exploits the overload by the fork *1. . . . Rb7*
78a)	Black traps the bishop by *1. . . . Kb7*
78b)	Black deflects the rook by *1. . . . e1/Q* +
79a)	White mates by *1. Nf6* ++ or *1. Ng5* ++
79b)	White skewers and deflects by *1. Rg8* +
80a)	White mates by *1. Rxg8* ++
80b)	White forks by *1. Qxe5* +
80c)	White mates by *1. Qxf8* ++
81a)	Black mates by *1. . . . Ra1* ++
81b)	Black gains a rook by *1. . . . Rd2* +
81c)	Black mates by *1. . . . Rxb2* ++
82a)	Black simplifies to a draw by *1. Nxa6 2. Nxa6 Bxb3*
82b)	White insures promotion by *1. Ne7*
82c)	White forks by *1. Ne7* +
83a)	Black mates by *1. . . . Qxh2* ++
83b)	Black mates by *1. . . . Qxh2* ++
83c)	Black mates by *1. . . . Bxf3* ++
83d)	Black mates by *1. . . . Qf1* ++
83e)	Black mates by *1. . . . Qxf3* ++
84a)	White mates by *1. Rc7* ++
84b)	White mates by *1. Re7* ++
84c)	White forks by *1. Nf6* +
85a)	White mates by *1. Rxf8* ++
85b)	White mates by *1. Qxf7* ++
86a)	Black discovers by *1. . . . Rf8* +
86b)	Black mates by *1. . . . Qg1* ++
86c)	Black mates by *1. . . . Qh1* ++
87a)	Black pins the rook by *1. . . . Be1*
87b)	Black promotes by *1. . . . d2*
88a)	White mates by *1. Qxg8* ++
88b)	White mates by *1. Qh6* ++ or *1. Qg8* ++
88c)	White mates by *1. Qh7* ++
89)	Black mates by *1. . . . Qh2* ++ or *1. . . . Qf1* ++
90a)	White shuts off the rook by *1. Bd5*
90b)	White shelters his king by *1. Kd6*
91a)	Black stops the a-pawn by *1. . . . Bd4*
91b)	Black stops the a-pawn by *1. . . . Bc5*
91c)	White controls d4 by *1. Ke4*
91d)	White controls c5 by *1. Kd5*
91e)	Black stops the pawn by *1. . . . Bd4*
92)	White establishes a passed pawn by *1. e6*
93a)	Black mates by *1. . . . Qe8* ++
93b)	Black mates by *1. . . . Qh2* ++
94a)	White mates by *1. Qg5* ++
94b)	White mates by *1. Qg5* ++
95a)	White mates by *1. Qb7* ++
95b)	White promotes by *1. a7*
96a)	White forks by *1. d7*
96b)	White pins by *1. Rb8*
97a)	White wins a rook or promotes by *1. Rd7* +
97b)	White promotes after *1. Rd8*
97c)	White forks by *1. Rd8* + and soon promotes

98a) Black mates by
1. . . . Qg3++

98b) Black mates by
1. . . . Qg2++

99a) Black mates by 1. . . . Rd1++

99b) White simplifies by 1. Qb7+

99c) Black shields the promotion
square by 1. . . . Nc1

100a) White boxes out by 1. Kb7

100b) Black makes a book draw by
1. . . . Kc8
or 1. . . . Kc7

Glossary of Tactical Terms

BACK-RANK MATE: A mate given by a queen or rook along the first or eighth rank. Also called a *corridor mate*.

BATTERY: Two pieces of the same color attacking along the same line.

BOOK ENDING: An endgame position for which there is a known best way to play.

DEFLECTION: The forcing of a defending piece from its post.

DISCOVERY: An attack by a stationary piece revealed when a friendly unit moves out of its way. Also called *discovered attack*.

DOUBLE ATTACK: Any attack against two separate targets simultaneously.

FORK: An attack by one unit against two enemy units at the same time.

GAMBIT: A voluntary sacrifice, usually of a pawn.

KING HUNT: A series of moves that chase the enemy king around the board until it is mated.

MATING ATTACK: A general assault against the king, leading to mate or significant material gain.

MATING NET: A position in which mate is forced.

OVERLOAD: A situation in which a unit cannot fulfill all its defensive commitments at the same time.

PILING ON: Exploiting a pinned unit by attacking it with additional force.

PIN: An attack on an enemy piece that shields a more valuable piece.

PIN OVERLOAD: Exploiting an overloaded piece by pinning it.

PROMOTION: Advancing a pawn to its last rank and changing it into a queen, rook, bishop, or knight.

REMOVING THE GUARD: Capturing or driving away a unit that is guarding another. Also called *removing the defender* or *undermining*.

SACRIFICE: Generally, the offer of material for another kind of advantage, such as initiative.

SHUT OFF: A line block that prevents an enemy unit from controlling the line.

SKEWER: The opposite of a pin. An attack on a valuable piece that by moving exposes another unit to capture.

STRATEGY: A general plan.

SUPPORT MATE: A mate given by a unit that is protected by another.

TACTICS: Immediate attacks and threats.

TECHNIQUE: Getting the most out of a position by precise maneuvering, with attention to nuances and subtle moves.

TRAPPED PIECE: A piece with no escape that can be attacked and captured, usually with advantage.

UNDERPROMOTION: Promoting a pawn to a rook, bishop, or knight, but not to a queen.

UNPIN: A counterattack that breaks a pin, gains time to break a pin, or ends a pin by eliminating or diverting a pinning unit.

X-RAY: A skewer attack or defense.

Index of Players

Ivanchuk:	Belyavsky 68, Torre 55
Ivanov, A.:	Fedorowicz 96
Ivanov, K.:	Shirazi 44
Judasin:	Luther 31
Kamsky:	Leveille 32
Karpov:	Belyavsky 59, Hjartarson 42, Salov 19, Seirawan 30, Yusupov 23
Kasparov:	Belyavsky 50, Illescas 37, Korchnoi 98, Kouatly 73, Salov 48, Short 71
Kinderman:	Maus 52
Koch, J.R.:	Wilder 93
Komarov:	Sakaev 38
Korchnoi:	Belyavsky 81, Kasparov 98, P. Nikolic 85
Kotronias:	Goldin 54
Kouatly:	Kasparov 73
Krasenkov:	Arbakov 18, Simic 86
Krysanov:	Cetverik 75
Kudrin:	Polugaevsky 60, Schroer 5
Kveinys:	Tonchev 7
Lanka:	Glek 49
Lerner:	Thorsteins 27, Vogt 67
Leveille:	Kamsky 32
Ljubojevic:	Portisch 16, Speelman 56
Lobron:	Greenfeld 90
Luther:	Judasin 31
Marjanovic:	Sermek 26
Maus:	Kinderman 52
Miles:	Alburt 43, Gruenfeld 20, Hennigan 41, Sokolov 3
Mohr:	Hoi 21
Murey:	Fedorowicz 11
Nikolic, B.:	Plchut 70
Nikolic, P.:	Hübner 9, Korchnoi 85
Nunn:	Christiansen 61
Peters:	Christiansen 69
Petursson:	Schlosser 91, Sherzer 99
Piket, J.:	Sax 76
Piket, M.:	Gheorghiu 2
Plachetka:	Balashov 10
Plchut:	B. Nikolic 70
Polgar, J.:	L.B. Hansen 8
Polgar, S.:	Suba 39
Polgar, Z.:	Sion 24
Polugaevsky:	Kudrin 60
Popovic:	Bagirov 92
Portisch:	Ljubojevic 16
Prie:	Psakhis 57
Psakhis:	Prie 57, Tolnai 4
Reyes:	Stohl 97
Rohde:	Brooks 80, Shipman 14
Sakaev:	Komarov 38
Salov:	Ehlvest 46, Karpov 19, Kasparov 48, Short 51, Vaganyan 77
Sax:	L. Hansen 65, Piket 76, Tseshkovsky 25, Vaganyan 22
Schlosser:	Petursson 91

Schmidt:	Sznapik 6
Schroer:	Kudrin 5
Seirawan:	Gulko 62, Karpov 30
Sermek:	Marjanovic 26
Sherzer:	Petursson 99
Shipman:	Rohde 14
Shirazi:	K. Ivanov 44
Short:	Illescas 84, Kasparov 71, Salov 51, Vaganyan 72, Yusupov 64
Sieglen:	Wessein 40
Sillman:	Christiansen 78
Simic:	Krasenkov 86
Sion:	Z. Polgar 24
Smyslov:	Chandler 33
Sokolov:	Anand 17, Miles 3, Van der Weil 53
Spassky:	Adams 35, Anand 82
Speelman:	Ljubojevic 56
Spraggett:	Yusupov 15, 79
Stohl:	Reyes 97
Strikovic:	Belov 95
Suba:	S. Polgar 39
Sulava:	Gauglitz 13
Sznapik:	Schmidt 6
Thorsteins:	Lerner 27
Tolnai:	Psakhis 4
Tonchev:	Kveinys 7
Torre:	Ivanchuk 55
Tseshkovsky:	Sax 25
Vaganyan:	Salov 77, Sax 22, Short 72
Van der Sterren:	Gelfand 89
Van der Weil:	Sokolov 53
Velimirovic:	Damjanovic 100
Vera:	Vilela 34
Vilela:	Vera 34
Vogt:	Lerner 67
Watson:	Burgess 1
Wessein:	Sieglen 40
Westerinen:	Garcia 87, Zaitzev 63
Wilder:	J.R. Koch 93
Yusupov:	Karpov 23, Short 64, Spraggett 15, 79
Zaitzev:	Westerinen 63

Index

on castled kings, 11, 63–93
defined, 11, 198
mating nets vs., 11
support, 200
on uncastled kings, 11, 37–62
mating nets (patterns; forced
mates), 10, 19–36
with bishop and knight, 15
defined, 10, 198
mating attacks vs., 11
sacrifices in, see sacrifices
triple attacks in, 59
Maus, So., 103
middlegame:
endgame vs., 47, 78, 136
opposite-color bishops in, 70–
71, 136
Miles, A., 23, 47, 81–82
Miles, T., 85
Mohr, S., 48–49
Munich, 168
Murey, Y., 32

National Open, 149–50
New York, N.Y., 74, 112
New York Open, 117–18
Nikolic, P., 29, 134, 158–59
nonmating attacks, see discover-
ies; forks; pins; skewers
Nunn, J., 119

Ohra GM Group, 165–66
opposite-color bishops, 43, 70–
71, 149–50
draws and, 78, 136
in middlegame, 70–71, 136
overloads, 143, 145–47, 151–52,
154–55, 160–62
defined, 11, 198
pin, 119, 123–24, 200

Paris, 32, 110–11
passed pawns, 67, 108, 153, 167
promotion of, 12, 175–182
patterns, see mating nets
pawn promotion, 12, 175–182
underpromotion in, 181–82

pawns:
in algebraic notation, 14, 16
passed, 67, 108, 153, 167
perpetual check, 22, 25, 104
Peters, J., 133
Petursson, M., 168, 181–82
pieces, notational designations
for, 14
Piket, J., 144
Piket, M., 22
piling on, 122, 198
pin overload, 119, 123–24, 198
pins, 33, 34, 74, 97, 115–30
defined, 11, 199
doubling of, 79–80
piling on of, 122, 198
skewers vs., 11
Plachetka, J., 30–31
Plchut, 134
Pogaska Slatina, 167
Polgar, J., 28
Polgar, S., 78
Polgar, Z., 53
Polish Championship, 26
Politiken Cup, 28
Polugaevsky, L., 117–18
Popovic, P., 169–70
Portisch, L., 41
position, material vs., 30–31, 34,
35, 60, 68–69, 81–82, 85–
87, 110–11, 119–21, 123–
124, 156–57, 161, 175–94
Prie, E., 110–11
promotion, 12, 175–182, 198
underpromotion vs., 181–82
Psakhis, L., 24, 110–11
Ptuj, 160
Pula, 175–76

queens:
positioning of, 27
rook and, 51, 58, 74
sacrificing of, 21, 28, 33, 43–
44, 72–73, 149–50

ranks, in algebraic notation, 12
Regional A Tournament, 92–93,
173–74

About the Author

BRUCE PANDOLFINI is the author of twelve instructional chess books, including *Bobby Fischer's Outrageous Chess Moves*, *Principles of the New Chess*, *Pandolfini's Endgame Course*, *Russian Chess*, *The ABC's of Chess*, *Let's Play Chess*, *Kasparov's Winning Chess Tactics*, *One-Move Chess by the Champions*, *Chess Openings: Traps and Zaps*, *Square One*, and *Weapons of Chess*. He is also the editor of the distinguished anthologies *The Best of Chess Life & Review*, Volumes I and II. Perhaps the most experienced chess teacher in North America, co-founder with Faneuil Adams of the Manhattan Chess Club School and director of the New York City Schools Program, Bruce Pandolfini lives in Manhattan.